Ali Dubyiah
and the Forty Thieves

Ali Dubyiah
and the
Forty Thieves

A Contemporary Fable

PRESENTED BY
John Egerton

NewSouth Books
Montgomery | Louisville
M M V I

NewSouth Books
P.O. Box 1588
Montgomery, AL 36102

Library of Congress Cataloging-in-Publication Data

Egerton, John.
Ali Dubyiah and the forty thieves : a contemporary fable / presented by John Egerton.
p. cm.
ISBN-13: 978-1-58838-202-3
ISBN-10: 1-58838-202-8
1. Bush, George W. (George Walker), 1946—Humor. 2. Bush, George W. (George Walker), 1946—Friends and associates—Humor. 3. Political corruption—United States—Humor. 4. United States—Politics and government—2001—Humor. 5. United States—Foreign relations—2001—Humor. 6. Satire, American. I. Title.
E903.3.E38 2006
973.931020'7—dc22

2006017458

First Printing August 2006

Printed in the United States of America

Do not veil the truth with falsehood,
nor conceal the truth knowingly.
—The Qur'an

Ye shall know the truth,
and the truth shall set you free.
—The Bible

Time's glory is to calm contending kings,
To unmask falsehood and bring truth to light.
—Shakespeare

One.

ong ago and far away, in a vast continental land called America, the capricious ruler of a hinterland province many days' travel from the capital plotted with his most trusted courtiers to take control of the entire hemispheric kingdom. This tribal ruler's name was George W. Fratbush, son of Wimpbush, a previous monarch. The younger Bush and a brother, Jeb Ambush, had always vied for the favor of their elders, but in starkly different ways. Jeb was agreeable, compliant, ingratiating; he yearned to please. George, the eldest of four sons, was stubborn, devious, self-indulgent, and irresponsible; he had no more conscience than a fish has feathers, and his character was as thin and pliable as a Pinocchio puppet.

In his youth (which stretched beyond the normal

two decades to three or more), young George bus-
ily cultivated his chosen self-image as an irreverent
playboy, a reckless thrill-seeker, a rake and a rogue
who always got his way. Being born to privilege
and possessing unlimited resources had done
nothing to inspire in him a sense of gratitude. On
the contrary, he was contemptuous of his parents'
generosity, disdainful of his given name (which was
the same as that of his father), and thoughtlessly
rude to his elders, always confident of their bound-
less capacity to forgive and forget.

George was the prodigal son. His loyalty, such
as it was, he bestowed only upon his closest friends,
the young men with whom he spent so much time
in drunken celebration of their manhood, their
vanity and venality, and their occasional sexual
conquests. He reacted proudly when hailed by his
middle initial, W, which he and his companions
pronounced "Dub'-yuh"—and when his disap-
proving parents told him it was undignified, the
irreverent manchild flaunted it, like a coxcomb or
a clown's cap.

In the fullness of time, both George and Jeb used
their wealth and visibility to gain power as tribal

warlords in two large and widely separated regions far from the national throne. The ineffectual king, Wimpbush, had hoped and expected that Ambush would succeed him as the continental sovereign, but Wimpbush himself was unexpectedly overthrown by a boisterous retinue of latter-day huns who formed a temporary army of convenience behind a new ruler, King Zip (himself a former regional chieftain known as Willie Bubba), who talked glibly but eloquently of progressive reforms. Their bitterly contentious rival parties—King Wimpbush's Publicans and King Zip's Sinners—hid their unprincipled thirst for power behind sober masks of decorum and propriety, even as they plotted continuously to conquer all rivals and rule with overwhelming force.

King Zip was eventually disabled by a scandal of complex dimensions that the Scribes and Pharisees summarized into a one-word headline: Zippergate. The scheming Publicans seized upon this opportunity to regain the throne, but to the surprise of everyone—especially old King Wimpbush—it was not Jeb Ambush or any of the other pretenders who ascended, but the amiably self-righteous jester, the slacker son and brother from the tribal outback in the far southwest.

The decisive battle for dominion over the vast continental kingdom came down to a dramatic clash between the cocksure but vacuous Dubyiah and his nemesis, the prevailing candidate of the Sinners, a densely brilliant tactician called Prince Al Bore. The campaign devolved into a supreme test of endurance, as bewildering as it was bloody, and the outcome remained in doubt for weeks. In the end, the kingdom's high court of judicial sages, headed by Sir William Inquest, ruled by a margin of just one vote that Fratbush would wear the crown. And so it came to pass that, at the dawning of the twenty-first century, the reign of Ali Dubyiah commenced—and when it did, America's slow and agonizing yet painfully precipitous descent into darkness, its long day's journey into night, began to gather speed, like a loose boulder that presages an avalanche.

The Fall of the American Empire began innocently enough, with Ali Dubyiah offering little in the way of new and different ideas (although he did swiftly grant large tax reductions to his wealthiest subjects). Months passed without a clear sign of his intentions. Some of his fellow Publicans, privately concerned about his capacity for leadership, were content to have him take long vacations at his estate in the hinterlands. The opposition Sinners complained loudly of his performance—but secretly, they were just as happy to have him engaged in a bit of manual labor, even as he took pains to explain to the Scribes that it was "hard work." Better he should be outdoors doing harmlessly destructive things, like clearing underbrush, they whispered, than in the throne room doing catastrophically destructive things, like saber-rattling and carving on social programs.

Dubyiah liked to think of himself as a decisive leader, but in truth he was an unnervingly erratic gambler who made big decisions impulsively, without a moment's hesitation or the slightest trace of doubt, no matter how serious the problem at hand. The notion that acts had consequences simply eluded him; he could not entertain the thought that he might ever be wrong, and even when proved so, he refused to admit fault or accept responsibility for his mistakes. His was the blissful certitude and arrogance of the "true believer," an affliction common among obsessively religious individuals. Some of the devout were altogether selfless and benevolent, of course, but many more were just the opposite: sanctimonious, judgmental, narrow-minded, self-delusive. Alas, Dubyiah was permanently encamped among the latter.

The rigid conviction and sense of entitlement that seemed to be fixed in young Fratbush's personality, in his very nature, had been greatly reinforced and magnified after he experienced a transforming religious conversion (an epiphany which, curiously, he referred to in a humorous and somewhat offhanded way as "my Damascus moment," even though there is nothing to indicate that he knew anything at all about the old Syrian capital). Whatever the source of its power, this episode turned Dubyiah into a professed follower of the early Middle Eastern Jewish mystic and prophet, Jesus of Nazareth, whose disciples had spread from Jerusalem across Europe and America over a period of some two thousand years.

It was fashionable among many Euro-Americans

of this Bush-age to stage elaborate public displays of their religious piety. These so-called Christians were by no means unique in this regard, for as we know from the long train of history, there have been Islamic brotherhoods of Muslims in thrall to the prophet Muhammad, and Jewish, Hindu, Buddhist, and other religious societies equally as imbued with the zealous certitude of a "chosen people" favored by "the one true God."

Had Dubyiah not drifted into politics as his profession, his religiosity might have been persuasive, at least superficially. But he was so shallow, and so incurious, that few who knew him well could imagine him as a philosopher or a theologian or a wise man. Some believed he was smart enough, but intellectually lazy, lacking the desire or the discipline to achieve genuine excellence as a true statesman and an inspirational leader of his people. He did have a certain narrowly channeled ambition, however, and an enthusiastic spirit that traced back to his schooldays, and on the strength of these, he gathered round him over the years a tight circle of partisan loyalists, sycophants, political handlers, and wordsmiths who were willing to do the hard and dirty work of political skullduggery at his bidding. Their unwritten covenant with him was mutually beneficial: He had what they most desired (wealth, influence, name recognition), while they, collectively, had all the knowledge, organizational ability, and technical skills that he sorely lacked. They deferred to him and followed his lead when the citizens were watching—but often, in private, these shrewd handlers shaped their simple-minded and malleable leader to their own aims and desires. Looking back, it is quite easy to see how such a hollow man, together with his band of rogue companions, would ride to notoriety as Ali Dubyiah and the Forty Thieves.

Two.

The transformation of Ali Dubyiah into an international advocate of aggression and empire-building came with the speed of light. On a brilliant autumn day mere months after the start of his reign in the new millennium, America was assaulted by a soulless band of homicidal fanatics. All of the stealthy murderers were radical religious extremists, all were Muslims, and all were native sons of a vast region loosely joined by the Arabic tongue. Their spiritual leader, and the mastermind of this heinous plot, was an estranged son of Arabian wealth and prominence who, quite blasphemously, slaughtered innocent people in the name of Allah. Osama bin Hiden was his name.

An arresting irony lurks here. All we are given to know of it is somehow bound up in these two facts: First, a connection lubricated by crude oil and filthy lucre had long existed between the American Wimpbush clan and the bin Hiden family of Arab potentates. And second, the lives of Osama and George the younger, or Dubyiah, reveal to us some illuminating parallels. Both were spoiled rich boys born to privilege in the middle of the twentieth century; both were contemptuous of their elders (and wasters of their wealth); both were sheltered as young men, receiving their formal education in elite institutions and traveling only within a narrow cultural orbit; both, predictably, became adults who manipulated truth to suit their own desires, without guilt or apology; and both came to power as dogmatic religious radicals certain that Allah, or God, had chosen them to lead the faithful against the infidels. In disposition and temperament, they were enough alike to be cousins, if not brothers (except that Osama seemed totally devoid of a sense of humor). Although they never met face to face, they seemed destined to become arch-enemies, each driven by an obsessive fear and hatred of the other.

After his schooling was finished, Osama left Arabia for a mountainous region called Afghanistan, where an Islamic militia known as the Taliban had been locked in an extended struggle to drive out an army of invaders from the kingdom of Russia, to the north. The Taliban was receiving assistance from far-off America, a bitter enemy of Russia. As a Taliban fighter, Osama helped the American representatives (most of whom belonged to a unit of spies they called "CIA") to handicap the invading soldiers in various secret ways—such as boosting the agricultural production of opium poppies and channeling the alluring byproduct, heroin, into the hands of young Russian soldiers, leaving tens of thousands of them hopelessly addicted. (In large measure because of American agricultural expertise, tiny Afghanistan would soon become the world's largest producer of opium poppies. Such an irony!)

Eventually, the Russians were forced to withdraw. Osama returned to Arabia, but his radical ways led to his forced separation from the bin Hiden family (though not from its riches), and finally to his expulsion from the country. The Saudi royal family, to which his own family was related, was closely allied with America, and Osama came to hate both peoples as "infidels" and "enemies of God." America had used military bases in Arabia to wage war on another Muslim land, Iraq (a war instigated by Ali Dubyiah's father, old King Wimp-bush). Osama bin Hiden, having once fought on the same side with America, now swore eternal hostility toward this powerful land. In the years preceding Ali Dubyiah's ascension to the American throne, Osama emerged as an international terrorist with a price on his head. This was the prelude to his stealthy assault upon America's proudest symbols of power in its glittering showcase cities.

Osama sent twenty of his followers on a suicide mission to America, and miraculously, all but one of them managed to get aboard four flying ma-chines—so-called airplanes—and force them to crash into tall buildings. Two of the planes exploded in New York, one in Washington, and the fourth elsewhere. Altogether, about three thousand inno-cent people died, along with the nineteen who were under Osama's spell. This day of infamy would go down in history as something called Nine-Eleven. (The twentieth terrorist, a man with the biblical

name of Zacharias, was arrested by agents of a
non-uniformed American police force known as
the FBI almost a month before Nine-Eleven, but
lack of vigilance by the agents' superior officers allowed this man, whose surname was Mouse-oui, to
conceal his connection to the murderous plot that
was about to unfold. Not until years later would
it be revealed that his timely identification could
have forestalled the attack.)

Up to that point, Ali Dubyiah had failed to
distinguish himself as a leader—but in the ashes
of this unspeakable crime, he and his den of plot-
ters found the theme for his reign: He would be,
in his own oft-repeated words, "a War President."
Dubyiah the warrior, the avenger, would not rest
until Osama the Barbarian was vanquished.

At first he called his counterattack a "crusade,"
unaware that in ancient times the Christians of
Europe had launched frequent pre-emptive strikes
against the Islamic multitudes in Byzantium, giving
these incursions the name "crusades"—bold acts for
the glory of the Jesus followers and the destruction
of the Mohammedans. Ali Dubyiah was reluctant
at first to surrender this "crusader" mantle, but

when he finally did, he donned instead the white hat and silver star of a fabled American hero figure, the "Wild West sheriff," and vowed to bring back the outlaw bin Hiden, dead or alive.

Within weeks, America turned its armed might upon a remote region of Afghanistan, high in the mountainous Asian rim, where Osama was thought to be ensconced. But the wily Arab was elusive, and the war dragged on with no sign of a conclusion. In the meantime, against the advice of many sages, Fratbush and his henchmen decided the moment was ripe, and a convenient excuse was at hand, for a land grab in the oil-rich heart of the Middle East. Forthwith, he launched an invasion into that part of Persia called Iraq—the region where the ruins of Baghdad and ancient Babylon remain to this day—for the stated purpose of preventing its dictator, Saddam Gomorrah (another former CIA collaborator), from attacking America with mighty weapons capable of causing mass destruction.

It had been barely more than a decade earlier that the erstwhile king, Wimpbush, had fought a war with Gomorrah, leaving Iraq crippled but its beastly ruler still uncaged. The cocky Fratbush ached to smite him, not so much to avenge his father as to prove to the world that he, Ali Dubyiah, was a great warrior—and a braver man by far than the weak and equivocating patriarch, Wimpbush. The desire to succeed where his father had failed was all the motivation Ali Dubyiah needed, but his courtiers were much more ambitious. Even before the kingdom's high court had declared Fratbush the new ruler of America, these stealthy kingmakers were scheming to bypass the Parliament of Nations, overthrow Saddam, liberate his subjects, seize Iraq's oil fields, silence any opposition, and begin to establish colonial hegemony over much of the Middle East. Iraq was to be the first link in that chain, they calculated; its army could be overwhelmed in a brief but intense blitz—and the cost would be borne by the vanquished land's own bottomless well of crude oil, so readily convertible into vast riches.

As the Fratbush regime had long known with a high degree of certainty, Saddam no longer had any weapons of mass destruction—but he was, by all accounts, an evil and universally despised dictator who had cold-bloodedly slaughtered his own subjects, and no one would mourn his demise. Moreover, one dead Gomorrah on display would be worth two bin Hidens on the run, and Osama was proving impossible to capture, whereas killing Saddam would surely be as easy as spearing fish in a barrel. And so, garbed in this besmirched cloak of honor, patriotism, piety, and false democratic idealism, the Ali Dubyiah regime cynically averted America's eyes from the painful image of Osama bin Hiden and Nine-Eleven and focused instead on Saddam Gomorrah and his nonexistent arsenal of deadly weapons.

It was here that the powerful Publican Guard around Ali Dubyiah came into clear view as the sinister force behind the throne. The Scribes recorded much of interest and notoriety about these men and women who became "the Forty Thieves" of America, named after the legendary Persian band of ancient times. Some had been faithful Wimpbush supporters back when the old king had invaded Iraq the first time, but most were new kingmakers and accomplices. Some lived in the open, others in the shadows—and, of course, there were many more than forty of them. Among the most controversial of these characters were:

- Dick Chaingang, second in command to Ali Dubyiah, a man whose cold gaze could turn fire to ice. Dubyiah, who had an annoying penchant for giving pet names to his associates, called Chaingang "The Mole," and, later, "Deadwood Dick" or "Bullseye," mocking his ineptitude as a hunter—much to the secretive subordinate's private displeasure.

- Donald Rumsfailed, or "Dr. Toughlove" to Dubyiah. Another hard-hearted bully, Rumsfailed ran the kingdom's military establishment with snarling disdain for the opinions or fortunes of others, including his own generals—and, of course, in a spirit of absolutism, certitude, and boastfulness that Dubyiah deeply admired.

- Paul Werewolf, "The Jackal," a sly and cunning man whose genius was in secret planning and policy-making. He drew up the blueprints for a new American empire that would rule the Middle East, and might eventually dominate the globe.

- John Sackcloth, the kingdom's principal over-seer of legal and moral orthodoxy, more rigid by far than the Ruler to whom he pledged allegiance. Sackcloth's pet name, whispered by the surreptitiously irreverent Fratbush—but only in the moral avatar's absence—was "Ashhole."

- Karl "Babyface" Machiavrovelli, the master-mind behind the throne, the most brilliant and diabolical of all the rogues in Ali Dubyiah's den of scoundrels. Time and time again, he outsmarted the hapless Sinners, and saved the Publicans from disaster. The Scribes were no match for him, either. Machiavrovelli—who, for some reason, the Ruler called "Ratwater" or "Turd Blossom"—delighted in his mastery over all the kingdom of America, friend and foe alike. Truly, he was Dubyiah's brain, but his loyalty to his sovereign was absolute.

These five held special powers. Sackcloth stepped out of the circle after a few years and was replaced by a young Dubyiah sycophant, Alberto Gonadez, and the Werewolf left to become a global money-changer, but the other three—the Mole, Dr. Toughlove, and Babyface—remained at Ali Dubyiah's side to the bitter end, and no others ever reached their level of power. Numerous figures, such as Colin O'Scoppy and Condi Pasta (both of whom served full terms as the nation's top diplomat), held exalted positions within the kingdom for a time, but they lacked the confidence to challenge decisions and the authority to compel changes in policy. Condi Pasta was the strongest and smartest of a cadre of women whose devotion to their leader was absolute, but no female—including the Ruler's one and only wife (whom he referred to as "the Librarian")—ever found the key to Ali Dubyiah's heart and soul.

Others in the band of thieves should be mentioned in passing—for their colorful names, if not for their questionable contributions to this powerful political machine. Parliament was the base for many of these ruffians and outlaws, among them Tom DeCeive ("Vader"), Bill Frisk ("Dr. Yes"), Trent Notmuch, Rick Sanctimonious, Phil Milligram, Zero Miller, Strum Dixie, Orrin Orrin ("Mormon in America"), F. James Senseburner, Newt Getrich,

Jesse Heist, Dick AWOL, John McCain'-Get-No-Satisfaction, and Mitch McCarnal—whose wife, Elaine Chaos ("Madame Lafarge"), was a castle-keep and a Dubya-girl whom he chose to be his secretary of labor).

There were numerous Scribes and Pharisees as well, including Grover Conquest ("Bathtub"), Rush Roquefort ("the Bloviator"), George Won't, Ann Filly ("Big Bad Blonde"), Bill O'Yeah?!, Ralph Greed ("Acolyte"), William Rhinestone, Phyllis Shagafly, Bob Novakaine, George ("I Spy") Tenant, Tony Bloke ("the Brit"), Ariel Assault, Ahnold Terminator, the justices Antonin Scareya and Clarence Judas, the clerics Mulla Jerry ("Teletubby") and Mulla Pat ("God's on line one," the clownish Dubyiah would say to him), Ollie Contra ("Simper Lie"), and the quintessential enabler, Jack ("the Ripper") Abramon, kingpin of the service providers who catered to the Haves and Have-Mores in return for favors.

And who could ever forget such marvelous thespians and quick-change artists as the Iraqi grifter Ahmad Chubbily, and the Arab opportunist Yessir Jihad, and General Tommy Hotdog, and Viceroy L.

Paul Tremor, and culture maven Karen Huge, and press liaison Scott ("Mouthpiece") McCome-Clean, and the hurricane song-and-dance duo of Mike ("Spook") Shirtoff and his show-dog Brownie, and an Amen Chorus (a quintet, actually) of avaricious and inharmonious monkeys: Seeno Lay, Hearno Ebbers, Tasteno Scrushy, Smellno Kozlowsky, and Touchno Stewart?

Unless my abacus deceives me, the soldiers of misfortune here named were sufficient to give Ali Dubyiah his band of Forty Thieves, with some to spare—and there were, as I have said, many more willing souls in reserve. Unlike the Persian band of thieves in ancient mythology, most of them showed little interest in gold and silver and precious stones. Reminiscent of an earlier gang of burglars—the oddly-named Watergate Plumbers, in the reign of King Richard the Cold-Hearted—this ragtag army of brigands and their callow king did not set out to steal material treasures. No, what Ali Dubyiah and his Forty Thieves coveted most obsessively was power, control, domination, privilege, ideological orthodoxy. And in pursuit of these things, they conspired to steal the liberty of the king's own people, using secrecy, spying, eavesdropping, and other invasions of privacy. They also stole hope and opportunity from those who struggled for independence and self-sufficiency in the backwaters of mainstream society. Posing as guardians of personal security, they stole the health, the jobs, the pensions, and the fundamental wellbeing of unsuspecting millions who lived under the wayward rule of King Fratbush. And finally, in the desert sands of old Persia, they stole the lives of uncounted tens of thousands of Iraqis—the just and the unjust, without distinction—and, most grievously for so many patriotic Americans, they gambled away (the same as stealing) the lives and limbs and spirits of multiple thousands of their own brave men and women, sending them to fight an unprovoked and unjustified war of aggression for cynically spurious reasons.

In quest of a global empire, Ali Dubyiah's cabal of ideologues used the cover of Nine-Eleven to impose their will upon other kingdoms. And yet, only a minority of Americans ever uttered a word of public protest or even cast a private ballot in opposition. Audaciously, Dubyiah declared war on terror (a demented mindset, not a nation or an entity), and then insisted that his war powers as Commander in Chief of America gave him full authority to do virtually anything he wished, in public view or clandestinely, without consulting the congress or the courts. It would take the king's own repeated excesses, and those of his furtive inner circle of keepers, to finally awaken the people from their slumber—and by then, it was almost too late.

Three.

There is a wise old proverb (some say it originated with an ancient biblical character called Adam): "Be careful what you wish for." Even as Ali Dubyiah and his band of Publicans were ensconced in the seats of authority throughout every branch and limb of government in the most dominant nation on earth, they coveted more power. Amazing, is it not? The only armed Goliath, with military outposts in a hundred countries besides its own, the originator and perpetrator of the dreaded nuclear option, the possessor of more battle-ready weapons of mass destruction (over ten thousand!) than existed at that time in all other nations of the world combined, the last remaining military superpower on the planet—this Ares, warrior son of Zeus, deliberately set out to increase its military might so massively that no adversary would ever dare to challenge its power and control.

Another old saying also comes to mind, this one not wise but foolish: "Might makes right." The audaciously chauvinistic and polemical Fratbush devoutly believed this truism. He must have dreamed that he was, if not Ares, then Alexander the Great, or Napoleon, so resolutely did he take up this mission as God's chosen empire builder. "God told me to strike," he explained later, "and I struck them."

His brain-trust kept telling him that this was a task for he-men, not girly-men; sometimes, they said, you had to lie, steal, cheat, even torture your enemies. Rumsfailed, the chief warlord, was his principal counselor in this regard, constantly repeating the mantra that "democracy is untidy— people break things, steal things, people get hurt." It was a mean and nasty job, this Dr. Toughlove acknowledged, but someone had to do it—and if you could not be brutal and cold-blooded when confronting the evil empires that were lurking out there, then you could not be truly serious about ending terrorism, and spreading democracy, and enforcing peace and freedom throughout the planet, and keeping a thumb on the scales of the international free market. Ali Dubyiah was easily persuaded. He liked clear-cut choices—black or white, never gray. His philosophy was simple: Always be forceful, banish all doubt, never ask for permission or, after the fact, forgiveness.

The decision to invade Afghanistan had been accepted by the vast majority of Americans as a proper and necessary response to Osama bin Hiden and the Nine-Eleven terrorists. Then, a year or so later, a smaller percentage—but still a majority—accepted Fratbush's argument that the same aggressive approach also had to be taken toward the Iraqi dictator, Saddam Gomorrah. He was poised to launch nuclear missiles at America, Dubyiah declared, "so we must strike them over there first, before they have a chance to strike us again over here. We can't afford to wait. The next smoking gun may be a mushroom cloud." Saddam, he declared emphatically, was closely allied with the bin Hiden terrorists who called themselves al Qaida—the Base—and in the post-Nine-Eleven world, this second Bush-king insisted, America must separate all nations into two camps, sheep and goats. "Either you are with us," the Ruler declared, "or you are with the terrorists."

In the march to war with Iraq, Dubyiah and his inner circle sought submissive allies, but vowed to fight alone, if necessary. They would not be dissuaded by threats or doubts or acts of appeasement; only unquestioning cooperation would suffice. No understanding of the people, language, and cultures of Old Persia would be necessary, they reasoned, because a new "Pax Americana" would soon prevail.

America's bold invasion would be characterized by the "shock and awe" of overwhelming force, after which the grateful Iraqi people would welcome the warriors in this "coalition of the willing" as liberators, and it would all be over quickly, and statues of Saddam Gomorrah would soon be replaced with tributes to the Bush-king. The zealous American leader fairly salivated in child-like anticipation of this moment of painless triumph. "Bring it on!" he exclaimed—which was an English colloquial expression meant to taunt an adversary.

(In Arabic, the word is a common expression, pronounced "Yalla!")

Indeed, it would be only a matter of weeks before Dubyiah the Great donned a warrior's garb and stood before a cheering throng of sailors on the deck of a ship at sea to declare that America and its allies had prevailed in Iraq, and that major combat operations there had ended. "The tyrant has fallen, and Iraq is free!" he exclaimed. A banner draped high above his head signaled victory: MISSION ACCOMPLISHED. Scribes who had been ferried out to the ship to record this joyous scene dutifully reported it in words and pictures, and soon all Americans saw before them this indelible image of a triumphant Bush-king in battle dress, his manner more like that of a boastful conqueror than a magnanimous victor.

Alas, the celebration would prove to be premature—closer to the beginning than the end of hostilities. Certainly there was shock and awe, but it did not come at the end of a six-week war of liberation paid for with oil revenues from the defeated Gomorrah and his Sunni Muslim dictatorship. Instead, America and all other nations of the world would be stunned to see how much would go awry in Iraq almost from the start, and for years to come. The cost in destroyed lives—American, Iraqi, and others—would be counted in the multiple tens of thousands of dead or maimed or mentally shattered; the cost in dollars (principal coin of the realm in those days) would soar into the multiple hundreds of billions.

As expected, Saddam's feared army proved to be too weak to resist the invaders, and his Baathist political party was easily fractured. But thousands of these men and women, sworn enemies of the invading force that had ravaged their country, faded into the civilian population to reinforce an underground resistance teeming with all manner of political, religious, ethnic, and criminal extremists—not just Iraqis, but fighters from throughout the Arab and Muslim diaspora.

This turn of events seemed to come as a great surprise to the invasion planners, whose confident expectation continued to be that all Iraqis would be overcome with thankfulness at their release from the clutches of the butcher Gomorrah. Looking on as roving mobs systematically pillaged the preserved history, art, culture, and archaeological wealth of this hallowed birthplace of civilization, the pre-emptive strikers were alternately amused, amazed, and appalled. Some of them derisively lampooned the mobs as "Ali Babas"—robbers and thieves—and compared them to ghetto dwellers who took advantage of civil disorder to loot and burn their own shops and villages. This only heightened the rage of many Iraqis, who returned the insult with their own chants: "America is Ali Baba! Robber! Thief!" Whether the people of Iraq loved Saddam, or loathed him, or lived in mortal fear of his return, the invasion had given them a powerful new focus, and they quickly vented their multifarious grievances against America and all the rest of "Western culture."

After some months in hiding, the fugitive Saddam was captured, and thus his genocidal rage against Shiite Muslims and ethnic Kurds in Iraq was finally and mercifully ended. But the country's three major population groups—Sunnis, Shiites, and Kurds—would gradually turn from fighting the invaders to fighting among themselves across religious and ethnic lines. All that had kept the motley horde of radical insurgents from a vicious and self-destructive civil war, ironically, was the continued presence of their common enemy, America, and its handful of co-invaders. As time dragged by with no peace in sight, and as the toll of casualties mounted, the terrible truth of Ali Dubyiah's folly was inescapable: What the impetuous Ruler had so recklessly set in motion was now energized by its own perpetual momentum, and no party or faction, least of all the Americans, could get off the spinning wheel of death and destruction, or make it stop spinning.

The most amazing and confounding development to emerge in the midst of these nightmarish hostilities was the collective decision of the American voters, a year or two after the invasion of Iraq was launched, to endorse and support the Fratbush administration for a second term in power. To be sure, the margin was narrow, and loudly disputed by many, but it was hardly as controversial as his first election contest, and this time the outcome did not hang in the balance awaiting judicial resolution, as it had previously. This time, George

W. Fratbush actually got more votes than his opponent—or so it was reported—and no hair-split-
ting judicial technicality was employed to declare
him the winner. (This eventuality brings to mind
yet another wise old saying: "In a democracy, you
get what you deserve.") The Bush-king regime had
succeeded in dividing the American people into
two bitterly hostile camps—one seeing nothing
but disaster in his every move, the other blind to
his every blunder. A condition of mutual contempt
between these factions had settled over America
like a noxious cloud almost from the very day he
ascended the throne, and it persisted—nay, intensi-
fied—throughout his tenure.

Nine-Eleven was the most grievous assault ever
perpetrated upon the proud American nation,
one that would not be overcome for generations,
centuries. Brave and innocent people died, and
the world wept in sympathy and compassion for
them. America's initial reaction—the pursuit of
bin Hiden and al Qaida—was widely deemed to be
justified, even though a greater number of innocent
Afghans would die there, along with many culpable

ones who boasted of their complicity in the mass
murder in New York. But then came the invasion
and occupation of Iraq, and as it stretched into
years, the reasons for such carnage evaporated like
a desert mirage. As reports of needless torture and
killing echoed across the ravished landscape, and
as vast amounts of money seemed not to smother
but to stoke the fires of hatred, and as Osama bin
Hiden remained a fugitive from justice, the specter
of a horrendous tragedy of mythic proportions
painfully unfolded before the shocked and enraged
nations of the world, by far the most of which had
expressed firm opposition to the Iraqi misadven-
ture before it commenced. The war of aggression
and occupation that so many had pleaded with
Ali Dubyiah not to start was now a killing field of
vengeful slaughter and ceaseless retaliation.

No connection could ever be found linking
bin Hiden and Saddam Gomorrah. Both were
Sunni Muslims, but bin Hiden's fundamentalist
extremism stood in sharp contrast to Gomorrah's
secular disregard for most things religious. Later
in the war, a Jordanian-born terrorist named Abu
Musab al-Zarkaddy proclaimed himself the leader

of an insurgent band called "al Qaida in Iraq"
and commenced a wave of brutal killings, but he
turned out to be more of a rival to bin Hiden than
an ally. Zarkaddy was eventually killed by American fighters; only then, when he was safely dead,
did Osama praise his indiscriminate butchery in
Iraq. A reward of twenty-five million dollars had
been publicly offered by the American military
command for Zarkaddy's elimination (and earlier
for bin Hiden and Gomorrah), but if the fighters
who killed him did, in fact, receive the bounty, it
was awarded quietly, without public notice.

The hope that the capture of Gomorrah or the
killing of al-Zarkaddy (not to mention the eventual
fate of the ever-elusive bin Hiden) would bring
peace to Iraq remained just that—a hope, one that
was bound to be dashed. Senseless killing continued unabated. Nor did the formation of an Iraqi
government or the gradual reduction of American
occupation forces prove to be firm steps toward
peace. Iraq was rife with a turmoil that bordered
on anarchy as the majority Shiites, the formerly
dominant Sunnis, and the ever-maligned Kurds
(also Muslims, but not Arabs) clashed with one

another, with the occupiers, with freelance militias and newly recruited police and military troops, all of whom had formerly been either loyalists or enemies of Saddam Gomorrah.

Yet even as the body count steadily mounted, Dubyiah glibly rambled on about "liberating fifty million people" . . . "protecting America from evil regimes" . . . "stopping the terrorists at the source" . . . "bringing democracy and hope to the oppressed" . . . "preserving and defending our moral values"—phrases that seemed the very antithesis of his actions. Iraqis no longer feared the wrath of Saddam—but far from being liberated, they found themselves trapped in a hellish and inescapable war zone where freedom was a cruel hoax and democracy a hollow mockery. As for moral values, Fratbush loudly proclaimed them, but his deeds fell far short of his words. He never acknowledged a single mistake in the march to war, never admitted that Saddam Gomorrah had no weapons of mass destruction and no alliance with bin Hiden. Worse yet, Ali Dubyiah never accepted any responsibility for all the death and destruction he had initiated, never attended a single fallen warrior's funeral, never even allowed photographs to be taken of their flag-draped caskets.

When it was revealed that torture was being used to loosen the tongues of some captured insurgents, the Ruler at first denied it, then admitted it, and finally blamed it on "a few bad apples" at the bottom of the military barrel. Later, it was disclosed that some Arab captives had been spirited away from Iraq and Afghanistan, or kidnapped off the streets of other nations not at war, and taken blindfolded and in shackles to yet another Arab or European country, there to be tortured in secret—a practice referred to ominously as "extreme rendition"—and once again, Fratbush denied it. Hundreds of these "enemy combatants" or "detainees" (never "prisoners") were taken to a remote dungeon on the island of Cuba—itself an enemy nation in America's eyes—and kept there in total isolation for years without being charged with or tried for any crime. (America's highest court eventually would halt this unconstitutional practice.)

In the war zones of the Middle East, innocent children, women, and old men often died in bombing attacks by Americans (and were classified as "collateral damage.") Brave American soldiers were killed or maimed because their vehicles had been insufficiently armored. The insurgents kidnapped and sometimes beheaded Americans and others working in Iraq. They sent suicide bombers into the streets to blow themselves up, killing dozens and scores of their own people in the process. Sunni and Shiite death squads systematically wreaked vengeance upon each other, to be followed by retaliation and then more vengeance, in a senseless pattern made familiar throughout history by Arabs and Israelis, Serbs and Croats, Hutus and Tutsis, Indians and Pakistanis, Turks and Greeks, Catholics and Protestants, Christians and Muslims. Death and dismemberment were as commonplace as sunrise and sunset. Lies were spread to conceal the horrors being perpetrated upon the innocent, be they civilian onlookers, so-called enemy combatants, or Americans trying to serve their country with fidelity and honor. All this and more took place month after month, year after year. Yet the American people, through their ballots or the machinations of their political representatives, repeatedly acquiesced in the malfeasance of King George, and never attempted to remove him from power, as they had tried but failed to do to his predecessor, King Zip, for a moral failing in his personal life. Neither Zip nor Dubyiah were paragons of virtue—but as was commonly remarked in those days, "When Zip lied, nobody died."

Because of Ali Dubyiah's hubristic arrogance, the reputation of this once-mighty nation as a positive force in the world was irreparably harmed. In the name of combating terrorism, American foreign policy was breeding new terrorists who used Iraq as a training ground for their evil deeds. Saddam Gomorrah, who had struck fear in the hearts of all when he was a dictator, was left to putter about angrily but harmlessly in his own garden plot in prison, a petulant captive puffing on his daily cigar as he awaited his trial—which, when it finally began, was quickly reduced to a boisterously chaotic spectacle and an interminable circus, with the demented ex-dictator as its ringmaster. Saddam lived on, but death was everywhere, and no one accepted the burden of it, choosing instead to blame it all on others.

Meanwhile, deep in the remote mountain

fastness of Afghanistan or Pakistan, the renegade religious fanatic Osama bin Hiden, perpetrator of so much destruction and terror, remained safely beyond the grasp of his pursuers. From time to time he sent taunting messages to his arch-enemy Ali Dubyiah, blaming him for the havoc and horror that was destroying Iraq and endangering the entire world. Dubyiah usually returned the insult, but did not linger on the subject, for it was the same as saying, "This evil one whom I swore to bring back, dead or alive, is not only alive but still at large, and free to menace mankind as he wishes."

If, as both of these powerful men so reverently professed, there lived, beyond space and time, a just and vengeful God who would someday appear on earth to judge the quick and the dead, it was by then abundantly clear that many others in addition to Saddam Gomorrah would be summoned to account for a burdensome chronicle of misdeeds.

Four.

Before he first came forward to seek the office his father had once held and then lost, George W. Fratbush was known in his western domain as a handsome, humorous, hail-fellow-well-met. His reputation as a light-hearted, fun-loving cheerleader for conservatism preceded him. Throughout his youth he had shown far more enthusiasm for playfulness than for a life of the mind, or a life of service, or a life of sacrificial commitment to anything or anyone outside his own narrow circle of self-interest. To aspire to scholarship, for example, or to aim for a career in the military or the ministry or medicine or law, or to strive for excellence in athletics or entertainment—such dreams as these had never seduced him. His years of schooling at the most exclusive institutions yielded little of value and nothing of originality, and his service in the National Guard was equally as undistinguished, marked more by unexplained absences than by any hint of skill, passion, or bravery. Selfless dedication to a calling or a cause was for young George a state of mind to be avoided at all costs. His elders, witnessing his lack of commitment and discipline, used their money and influence to smooth his way over the rough spots, reasoning that without their help he would fail miserably, causing great embarrassment to the family.

As he began his campaign to reclaim the throne in the name of his father (more precisely, in his own name, for he had been, like the hero of a novel by the Bolshevik-turned-capitalist writer Ayn Rand, "born without the ability to consider others"), young "Dub-yuh" took pains to be seen as "a compassionate conservative," a leader whose captaincy would inspire many private and faith-based initiatives to augment the government's assistance to millions of its subjects, especially the working poor. He would steer the nation toward peace and cooperation, Dubyiah vowed; more than that, he promised to be a careful steward of the environment, a wise protector of the health and education of the people, and a good neighbor to America's friends and allies around the world.

That was the compassionate part. As for the conservatism, his most salient priorities included cutting taxes, turning some government programs over to private enterprise, and loosening the rules and regulations that applied to both "clean" and "dirty" industries, from banking and insurance to timber and coal. In the area of foreign policy, Fratbush disclaimed any interest in "nation-building," saying that empires were an old and outdated concept, an idea whose time had gone, and he had no desire to return to it. Another mark of his conservatism was apparent in his view of the judicial system. It would be his aim, he said, to appoint only "strict constructionists" to the federal courts—men and women who would respect the constitutional rights of individuals and states of the union by hewing to the letter of the law and not attempting to "legislate from the bench."

As fate would have it, judges were thrust into the national spotlight before Fratbush was even declared the winner of the popular election—indeed, it was judges who rendered that declaration. Specifically, it was the high court of the land, in a five-to-four decision, that overrode the authority of one state's judiciary and issued a ruling based not on any language in the Constitution but on a convoluted philosophical rationale that was a model of precisely that which had been rejected: judges of the nation's highest court attempting to legislate from the bench.

This was the unmistakable signal—if one were truly needed—that the new Bush-king would seldom be who he said he was or do what he said he would do, but rather just the opposite, like a fairyland looking-glass figure: left is right, right is left, up is down, in is out. As with the wars he would start and the friendly nations he would turn into adversaries, this man with a king's ego and a jester's élan seemed almost destined to preside over a domestic agenda as confounding and contradictory—and as destructive—as his foreign policy.

He and his hand-picked cabal were determined not to continue with business as usual in the conduct of government. In fact, they were plotting a massive deconstruction of governmental programs and services on the home front long before Dubyiah had even been anointed by the high court.

His tenure began as expected, with tax cuts for the wealthiest citizens, but as time passed, the Bush-king angered many economic conservatives with his undisciplined spending habits. Whereas in campaign speeches he had gleefully lambasted the Sinners as "tax-and-spend liberals," he would in time be criticized by them—and even by some of his fellow Publicans—as a "borrow-and-spend conservative." In such domestic fields as education, agriculture, and health care, he increased the government's expenditures and its oversight, and after Nine-Eleven, he created a massive new Department of Homeland Security. Within a very short time, these expanded outlays at home, together with the costs of war, turned a huge budget surplus that had been left to him by King Zip into an even larger budget deficit.

Reading from prepared texts to carefully screened audiences of avid supporters, Fratbush glibly parroted many of the things that economic conservatives wanted to hear from him—about free-market economies, deregulation, privatization, globalization, outsourcing, and what he liked to call "the ownership society" (and others called "an aristocracy of wealth"). But the economists soon were made uneasy by the extent to which the Ruler's words failed to match the actions of his government. The combination of massive public spending, burgeoning debt, tax relief for the rich, and reckless borrowing from abroad (especially from former adversaries, such as Japan and China) stirred deep concern among many fiscal experts. They noted with alarm that Fratbush had borrowed more money from foreign sources in his first term as Ruler than all the previous presidents combined, since the birth of the Republic! Was he a big-spender wolf in big-saver clothing? Could it be, they worried, that in his heart, Dubyiah secretly shared his father's disdain for (they would say, his complete misunderstanding of) their so-called "supply-side" or "trickle-down" monetary theories? (Old King Wimpbush had his own choice name for the philosophy: "voodoo economics.")

With so many critics of his foreign and domestic policies abounding, Ali Dubyiah might not have weathered the storms of discontent that had begun to gather around him, had it not been for two factors. The first, of course, was Nine-Eleven, which brought an outpouring of sympathy for the Commander-in-Chief (his public approval rating leapt overnight from five of every ten Americans to nine of every ten). The attack rallied the citizenry to stand together, and focused the nation's attention on defense and protection, and made people more tolerant of such things as long transportation delays, soaring oil and gasoline prices, government surveillance, secrecy, limits on civil liberties—and, most particularly, war.

The other lifebuoy that kept him afloat was the "third dimension" of conservative Publican politics: the oddly-named "Religious Right." (Did that mean right as opposed to wrong, or right as the opposite of left, or both, or something else?) Scholars would long ponder the conservative spirit of old America, but few would fully grasp the meaning and consequences behind the rationale: that unrestricted wealth was both the carrot and stick of sustained growth in a capitalist society. All blessings flowed from a triangular source of money and power. Some described it as a three-legged stool, others as a trinity, still others as "the three C's" of hierarchical European hegemony: the Crown (an expansive, imperial force), the Corporation (from which the economic conservatives held forth), and the Cross (religious, patriotic, and secretive in nature).

This third realm was the domain of radical conservatives who sought government power in order to enforce their social agenda—precisely the reverse of earlier reformers, whose mission it had been to build a wall of separation between church and state in order to protect the people's freedom to worship as they pleased. Throughout Dubyiah's reign, the Religious Right was his safety valve and his most dependable support group (more faithfully so than the rich, whom the Ruler loved more for their money than anything else, even as he publicly praised them as "my base, the Haves and the Have-Mores").

It may have been his own deeply suppressed sense of inadequacy that caused him to avoid intimate contact with any except those who made up his innermost circle (a circle that excluded all of his blood relatives). With everyone else, including conservative intellectuals, wealthy contributors, and even right-wing religious leaders whose support had assured his electoral success, Fratbush was secretly ill at ease, lacking in confidence, and always happier to be leaving than entering direct engagement with them, except in the briefest and most superficial encounters.

The Crown harked back to the era of European empires, when Britain, France, Spain, and other nations laid claim to vast territories they had reached by sea, wrested from the native inhabitants, and forthwith exploited. Fratbush was probably speaking truthfully, before he became Ruler, when he declared that he had no interest in empire-building. He was, at heart, a stay-at-home sort of fellow, not especially aggressive or competitive or curious. It was not until later, when his inner sanctum of counselors pushed their plan for global economic and military dominion, that the Bush Doctrine emerged to define his regime. Their grand vision fused two of the three C's—the imperial Crown and the multinational Corporation—into an invincible global powerhouse. (You could think of it as Bush, Incorporated.)

But that force, in and of itself, was not sufficient to conquer the world, or America, or even the Publican Party. There was one more essential factor, another necessary piece to complete the picture: that third C—the Cross. In earlier times, the three had worked hand in glove—as, for example, when Spain sent explorers to this "New World," as they called it, in about 1500. The Spanish king and queen, together with the Catholic Church and various private interests, cooperated in the conquest of aboriginal people, claimed their land, and extracted from it whatever valuable resources it contained, whether gold or jewels or spices, the bounty of which was then divided among the three C's to their mutual satisfaction.

America was one such frontier. Coveted by all the European powers, it was vied for by three most especially—France, Spain, and Great Britain—and in the end, it was Britain that prevailed. For almost two centuries, the colonies that would become America were kept in line by the British Crown and its subsidiary trading companies. Significantly, no

religious institutions were a formal part of that ar-
rangement (though some states nurtured piety more
than others, and the king did routinely declare, in
a meaningless and perfunctory nod to history, that
he ruled "by the grace of God"); indeed, it was to
escape religious oppression that many colonists
came to America in the first place. And, when they
finally rebelled against the British monarch (an
earlier King George, unrelated to the Bush-kings)
and won their independence, these "new Americans" took great pains to assure that their country
(which they formally called the United States of
America) would stand on its own as a completely
separate and independent nation. Neither Crown
nor Cross nor Company would govern; only the
people would, by a count of votes and majority rule.
Furthermore, the people's elected representatives
would themselves be subject to periodic review
by the voting public, and there would be, as well,
other safeguards against tyranny, such as a process
called "checks and balances." This meant that an
elected leader, called the President, and elected
representatives, collectively called the Congress,
would interact, and when disputes arose between

them, a third entity, called the Courts, or the Judiciary (appointed, not elected), would mediate their conflicts and resolve their differences.

It was, on the face of it, a very clever and effective system, but by the time of the Bush-kings, the framework was beginning to show the need for some repair. No one any longer used the old language: Cross, Crown, Company (or Corporation). New alliterations had modernized the concept, even though the meaning had not changed. Now the trinity was called "the Faith, the Flag, and the Fortune 500," or "Piety, Patriotism, and Plutocrats." There had emerged, in the culture-endangered and character-challenged world of the late twentieth century, an ever-widening religious revival that manifested itself in numerous ways, both positive and negative. In America, this spiritual awakening led to greater cooperation and tolerance between the two main currents of Christianity—Catholic and Protestant, as they were called—and also between Christians and Jews, and between those faiths and fragments of other religious cultures, including Buddhism, Hinduism, and Islam. But as ever in the course of history, the powerful institution

of religion was like a two-edged sword—it could
cut to cleanse, purify, and heal, and it could also
cut to subdue, dominate, and control.

By the Bush-king era, religion was once again
a presence to be reckoned with in many parts of
the world (especially was this so in America and
the Middle East), and political power gravitated
toward those who learned to integrate elements
of the spiritual into their more mundane and
secular ventures. Fratbush—King George the
Second (actually, the Fifth, if you count back to
Britain's George the Third, the one who provoked
the American Revolution)—lacked the intellectual
discipline and motivation, by himself, to graft those
wings onto the same bird, so to speak, but his trusted
courtiers—Chaingang, Rumsfailed, Sackcloth,
Machiavrovelli, and others—knew how vital that
objective was. (Of that quartet, only Sackcloth
wore his faith on his sleeve, but all four were adroit
political manipulators of religious institutions.) It
was their collective shaping of the Bush-king per-
sona over time that made him palatable to both
camps: the international/intellectual/libertar-
ian/economic conservatives, on one hand, and the

religious/patriotic/Christian/social conservatives on the other.

Of all these movers and shapers, Karl Machiavrovelli was by far the most important; he held the keys to the Bush-kingdom. From his own experiences as a youth in the shadow of the Mormon Church, and at college, "Babyface" had made a liberating discovery: that neither social nor economic conservatism, by itself, could carry the day in American politics. In the long run, the only way to prevail over the liberal spirit on which the nation had been founded was to effect a marriage of convenience between the two conservative camps: cool, calculating, cerebral money-changers on one side, and emotional, hot-blooded, hierarchical Christian soldiers on the other. The aim was not to yield advantage to either side, but rather, to stand between them and make both bend to a third will.

The smooth-faced, bespectacled "Choirboy Karl" was the only courtier with the intellectual dexterity to do that. The others were too ideologically enmeshed, or too distrustful of religious zealots, or too mesmerized by money, whereas he was a chameleon, able to change robes with ease.

He had become a poseur, a master impersonator:
He was Bush's brain, without benefit of a college
degree; he was hailed as a sage on matters of faith
and values, but his own religious affiliation, if any,
was not publicly known; he posed as an aggressive patriot, though he had evaded the draft in an
earlier war; he was a fierce critic of "government
meddling," except when he wanted to suspend
people's rights in order to punish "desecration"
of the American flag, or prevent the sale of birth
control drugs, or sanction prayer in public schools,
or give the state authority over doctors and fami-
lies as they grappled with heart-rending personal
decisions at the gateways of life and death. It is
impossible to imagine Ali Dubyiah ever winning
public office without the counsel of his intimate
friend and confidant, the one he delighted in calling "Turd Blossom." Without the legerdemain
of this shadowy figure, this puppeteer, the easily
distracted and intellectually challenged Ruler was
as helpless as an unclothed emperor, as useless as
a discarded scarecrow.

Until then, it had always been the economic conservatives who wore the mantle of the Publican Party. They had the money, and it spoke a loud and clear message to the faithful. But a rising conservative protest against the erosion of traditional values and moral standards was beginning to be heard in the late twentieth century, and some astute social engineers saw in this trend an opportunity to build a new political majority. Machiavrovelli was foremost among them. He perceived that a leader who could talk the talk of Big Money and walk the walk of Big Morality would be almost unbeatable in any contest based on majority rule. And, he had an ideal candidate in mind: a man with a marketable family name, corporate ties, political experience, and personal wealth; a once-besotted social derelict whose behavior had been radically altered by a religious encounter; a handsome and humorous fellow with an informal manner, an impulse for simplistic reasoning, an instinct for survival, and the ability to stay focused on a plan of someone else's devising. This candidate, of course, was George W. Fratbush.

And so, with the ever-faithful Babyface at his

side, like Sancho Panza in the shadow of Don Quixote, the provincial warlord had come riding up out of Texas in a swirl of prairie dust and pomposity, primed to take control of America. He cut a dashing figure, this lanky, sandy-haired product of Ivy League finishing schools who wore rawhide gloves to conceal the smooth softness of his hands. He was no longer "young George"; he was Dubyuh, and he affected the slow-motion swagger of a snuff-dipping "wild-West" cowboy, the new-money smirk of an oilfield wildcatter, and the steady, blue-eyed gaze of a true believer, whether the seduction was brown liquor, a well-turned calf, the wrath of God, or the rectitude of the Publican Party. His masterful underling had taught him many things, but one lesson was paramount: The combination of standard Publican politics (which was all about money) and new-age piety (which was mainly about numbers and power) was the figurative equivalent of an automatic assault weapon in his hands, and if he could learn when and how to use it, he would be invincible.

With two terms as a territorial governor to serve as his basic training, Ali Dubyiah arrived in

Washington determined to deliver to the Religious Right at least a few of the victories they had been seeking in vain for almost half a century. These goals had little or nothing to do with economic or political matters, in any formal sense, but instead were rooted in the primacy of biblical literalism in both private and public life. Some zealots hailed them as "a new Bill of Rights," or as "God-inspired additions to the Ten Commandments" that the biblical prophet Moses had handed down (on stone tablets, some said) many millenia ago. Among the new rules were these:

- recognition of the United States as a Christian nation;
- public funding for private and religious schools;
- compulsory Bible-reading and prayer in public schools;
- government funding of "faith-based initiatives" as an alternative to public social services;
- a ban on all abortions (as terminated pregnancies were then called);
- criminalization of individual decisions to

determine the viability of life, especially in its beginning and ending stages;

- criminalization of all sexual intercourse except that of heterosexual married couples attempting to procreate;
- legal definition of marriage as a formal religious union between two consenting adults, one male and the other female;
- legal sanction for the killing (otherwise known as execution or capital punishment) of certain individuals convicted of major crimes (Fratbush, when he was a territorial governor, signed warrants ordering the execution of more than one-hundred and fifty convicts);
- strict government control of research and experiments in all fields of science and medicine bearing upon human reproduction;
- sanction of Christian displays on government-owned property;
- protection of the American flag from any use deemed unpatriotic;
- tighter limits on the exercise of free speech;
- strict censorship standards in television and movies;

- unrestricted private ownership of firearms, regardless of size or power;
- a generally more punitive standard in matters of crime and punishment.

These were the core elements of the Christian Right agenda—"our family values," some called them, or "our moral principles," or "the foundation of our religious heritage." Indeed, practically everything about the list bespoke religion, though a few items had a more patriotic or military focus. Far from protecting the wall of separation between the church and the state, the clear intent was to completely destroy that wall. Each of these goals required a more aggressive government role in enforcing personal behavior. Taken together, they constituted a return to a Christian state, as when Cross and Crown dominated kingdoms throughout Europe centuries earlier.

Almost without exception or qualification, the new Ruler endorsed these measures and promised to work for their passage. As with other promises he made to various special-interest constituencies, this one was weak on the delivery end—but the promises

alone were enough to bring social conservatives to
the Publican Party as never before, and in tandem
with the fiscal conservatives, they produced a new
majority more potent than any previously enjoyed
by the right wing of American politics.

In the wake of the Nine-Eleven atrocity, George
W. Fratbush had been briefly paralyzed by the stun-
ning shock of such an unspeakable reality. He was a
man without a plan, a beleaguered leader forced to
witness his own world aflame. But within that ring
of fire there glowed a spark of opportunity, and at
the urging of his close counselors, he reached for
it. "This is our chance," they said. "Under cover
of this atrocity, we can avenge the earlier Gomorrah embarrassment in Iraq, seize his country from
him, liberate his people, corner the market on oil,
and begin the colonization (or should we call it
the democratization?) of the Middle East." In that
moment of peril, once he had regained his com-
posure, George W. Fratbush owned the permission
of more than nine in every ten Americans to do
virtually anything he wished with the power of his
office. "In an ironic way," his man Babyface told
him, "this diabolical Osama bin Hiden, intending

to deliver a mortal blow against us, has in reality done us a favor." The smooth-faced one smiled like a cat with a mustache of canary feathers. "Open sesame!" he chortled.

In that fleeting instant, the future of the world was in Ali Dubyiah's hands. He and he alone had the authority—and the responsibility—to save the earth from the depredations of evil and ignorant people. The choice was his: peace or power.

Five.

Years later, when he looked back upon his career in public service, George W. Fratbush must have felt a deep and abiding melancholy, as if he were adrift in a slough of remorse and regret. But then again, perhaps not; he was never one to entertain doubt. So deep was his sense of certitude and rectitude that such emotions as remorse, regret, contrition, and repentance rarely stirred within him—and when they did, as when he had his "Damascus moment"—they seemed almost out of character. If one were to compile "A History of America in the Age of Fratbush," it would read like a grand jury's painfully unrelenting and inescapable indictment—but the ever-sanguine Ruler had an uncanny ability to make the facts serve his own preconceived notions of right and wrong, truth and fantasy. In all probability, he went to his grave defending himself as "the Liberator of Baghdad" and "the Father of Democracy in the Middle East."

Fratbush had reacted to the heinous and cowardly Nine-Eleven attack as almost any leader except a pacifist would have, and for that he would be remembered with sympathy, if not praise. But then, in defiance of millions of people worldwide who marched in protest and pleaded with him to step back, he had proceeded to call down the military wrath of America upon Saddam Gomorrah (a deserving beast, if ever there was one). The brutal dictator's long reign of terror ended quickly enough, but Iraq's citizens were in no condition to celebrate; it was they who suffered most grievously from the American assault. Of the twenty-five million people that Ali Dubyiah boasted he had liberated there, perhaps a million were direct casualties— dead, injured, forced to flee—and the rest could only look on helplessly as their country collapsed in ruins all around them.

Intent upon raising up a showcase democracy

there, the occupying forces went immediately to work rebuilding what they and Saddam before them had so recently destroyed. Tens of billions of dollars were spent on reconstruction, so much that at times it seemed that a competition was being waged between the destroyers and the developers. In Baghdad and other urban centers, scenes of utter surreality unfolded continuously, even simultaneously, day in and day out, month after month, in a deadly theater of the absurd: bombs exploding in mosques and markets, oil fields blazing, blinding sandstorms astir, freshly butchered bodies found stacked like cordwood, battles raging across the tombs of old cemeteries, wedding parties turned into funerals, schools and clinics closing and opening and closing again, a constant cacophony of sirens, explosions, shouting, wailing. Darkness descended upon cities with no dependable sources of electric power or running water, and no place was truly safe, not even in broad daylight.

But some things did get fixed: the American Embassy, for example. It was the only reconstruction project in the country that stayed on schedule, and the only place where electrical power, running water, and sewage disposal never ceased to function.

The population of Iraq was roughly equal to that of Nepal, in the Himalayas, and in land mass, it was smaller than Morocco or Sweden—yet there, in a heavily fortified district called the Green Zone, in the heart of Baghdad, America carved out one hundred hectares (an area larger than the Vatican City that once dominated Rome, Italy) to build a fortress that would serve as its embassy. It was the largest in all the world, and by far the most expensive (almost a billion dollars!). It dwarfed the palaces of the vile and vain Gomorrah, and as a monument to extravagance, it even rivaled one of the "Seven Wonders of the World," the ancient city of Babylon, with it fabled hanging gardens, which King Nebuchadnezzar had built on the banks of the Euphrates River south of Baghdad more than twenty-five hundred years earlier, and which now bore the ravages of recent war as well as antiquity. The American Embassy and the Green Zone were visual symbols of a neo-colonial empire imposed upon another country in the slandered name of liberty, freedom, and democracy.

There was no way that history could ignore the magnitude of the disaster Fratbush had precipitated in Iraq; reminders of it were everywhere, strewn across the landscape. As the months turned to years, the Bush-king's own countrymen and women finally had to confront a grim reality thrust upon them by the war: In spite of the cost in American lives (more than three thousand casualties—fatalities or critical injuries—annually), and money (about a hundred billion dollars a year), this nation's military forces would remain in Iraq, risking their lives for peace, long after Dubyiah had retired to his hinterland estate—and yet there would be no peace, only perpetual civil war and cross-border clashes with neighboring regimes. This international bloodbath would last longer than the historic world war of the mid-twentieth century. In fact, many years after the peak force of about two hundred thousand soldiers, sailors, airmen, and private security personnel had been withdrawn from Iraq, about thirty thousand troops would remain, posted indefinitely at a few "enduring bases" around the country, or in the embassy compound. Another half-dozen American air bases were strategically located within striking distance, in such nearby countries as Qatar, Turkey, Kuwait, and Kyrgyzstan. The "War President" had let loose the War Genie in the Middle East, and it could no more be contained than smoke could be coaxed back into a bottle.

Without a doubt, on the fateful eve of America's premeditated assault in Iraq, the choice had belonged to Ali Dubyiah—peace or power—and sadly, like so many rulers before him, stretching back into the haze of history, he had chosen power. The planning and preparation had been ongoing since Nine-Eleven. He had long since decided on war; the only question was whether any eventuality could make him reconsider. None ever materialized. The die was cast. Resolutely, he launched the war, feeling the guiding hand of God on his shoulder. And so it is written: "The sins of the fathers are visited upon the sons, world without end, amen." History is no respecter of persons.

notwithstanding, it might still seem excessively partisan and mean-spirited—rather like flogging a dead horse—to lay all this blame at the feet of Ali Dubyiah. As many faults as he had, it was impossible to think of him as a genocidal maniac, like Attila the Hun or Adolph Hitler or Joseph Stalin—or like Saddam Gomorrah. No, it was much easier to think of Fratbush as a merchant, or a baker, or a youth services coordinator—friendly, cordial, fun-loving, church-going, never missing a civic club luncheon or a community fund-raiser, a regular at the coffee-shop roundtable where the leading Publican men of the town discussed current events. Few who knew him casually ever claimed that "Dub" was not an all-around fellow—"a nice guy," in the common parlance.

And (on the domestic front, at least) he had done some good things, admirable things. In his personal life, he had publicly renounced the use of alcohol, tobacco, and other addictive drugs, after being cited for some illegal behavior earlier in life. He was thought of by those close to him as a loyal friend, and he rewarded loyalty in others. He was generally assumed to be a faithful husband to his beloved Librarian, and a supportive father of their twin daughters. And if it was true, as was occasionally rumored, that the twins had overindulged in alcohol and crudely misbehaved at various parties and social gatherings of carefree youths, what parents could honestly claim not to have faced such challenges themselves? Words of wisdom from the ages: "There, but for the grace of God, go us all."

And further still, to give him his due, this second Bush-king sometimes took honorable but unpopular positions on controversial issues—as, for example, when he appointed to the Supreme Court two men of deeply (some would say extremely) conservative judicial philosophy, and boldly called upon the upper house of senatorial Lords to approve his choices. (One of these jurists had been hurriedly summoned to take the place of a previous Fratbush nominee of dubious independence from his persuasion; she had abruptly withdrawn her name from consideration when the Lords grew restive about her manifest lack of qualifications.) Most of the President's adversaries in the Sinner Party criticized his two court nominees as excessively partisan jurists, but they were intelligent and capable men, and it was his prerogative as Ruler to make such choices. Dubyiah taunted the Sinners by daring them to reject his nominees, but they lacked the nerve to attempt it. (Alas, the feeble objections raised by Sinners to the two men Fratbush appointed to the high court were soon borne out in several narrow decisions, joined by the new justices, that further shifted the federal balance of power away from the legislature and the courts, to the advantage of the executive. A solid conservative majority also made it harder for people of modest means to compete for political office, easier for states to put convicted capital offenders to death, and easier still for political parties in power to reconfigure voting districts to their advantage. A majority of the court did rebuke Fratbush when he claimed authority to bring imprisoned "enemy combatants" before extra-legal military tribunals without recourse to the most basic rules of law—but his two appointees sided with the two resident arch-conservatives, Antonin Scareya and Clarence Judas, on the losing side in that case.)

On another matter of great importance and controversy, Fratbush gave a tentative nod of approval to a class of immigrants who had entered America illegally, seeking work opportunities not available to them elsewhere. Against the strong opposition of many leaders in his own Publican Party, Ali Dubyiah declared that these immigrants were doing hard work that most Americans shunned (and doing it, he might have added, for less money—as day laborers, housemaids, and even soldiers serving in the wars, where they suffered and died in proportion to their numbers); for these contributions, the Ruler said, they should be allowed to pursue a legally approved path to citizenship, with all the benefits and obligations that entailed. (Coincidentally, perhaps, this was also the position taken by the nation's large business and commercial interests, which put great stock in a simple equation: profits rise in inverse proportion to the fall of labor costs.)

Having spent much of his youth in a region that bordered the lands of Mexico, "El Dubya" seemed genuinely to like the people, culture, language, and food of that ancient society of Indian and Spanish "mestizos," and in his benevolently paternalistic way, he thought of himself—and was regarded by many others—as pro-immigration. (By his own rigid standard, you will recall, there were only two choices on any issue: right or wrong, with us or against us.) Immigration was not a problem that

Fratbush could force to a satisfactory resolution
on his own, but he seemed at first to lean toward
the side of openness on this issue. Then, as a wave
of anti-immigrant reaction swept through the far
right flank of the Publican Party, El Dubya began
to fall in line with them; reinforcements were
rushed to the Mexican border, and construction
began on a high wall projected to follow the entire two-thousand-mile boundary (after which the
four-thousand-mile border with Canada would be
addressed). It was all in the interest of "national
security"—and almost all empty rhetoric for the
benefit of Anglo-Saxon nativists, isolationists,
"fortress America" extremists, and other Publican
reactionaries whose votes the party coveted in the
last election on Fratbush's watch. Immigration was
a conflict as old as the country itself—and, almost
by definition, beyond settlement—which perhaps
explained why the Ruler and Congress talked big
but did little to change the status of more than ten
million uncertified immigrants.

The Bush-king liked to leave work at a decent
hour, eat dinner at home, watch a little televi-

sion, and get to bed early, but the job of being America's Ruler forced many demands upon him: too much reading, talking on the telephone, posing for pictures with important people, making speeches, presiding at meetings, delegating authority. Worse yet, all the extra work seldom yielded good results. It seemed to him at times that something was always going wrong.

Numerous issues in the broad field of commerce and trade followed the Ali Dubyiah government like a dark shadow. There were massive corporate scandals, some involving executives who were Fratbush friends and campaign supporters. Besides stealing large sums of money, these executives were responsible for decisions that redounded to the discredit of themselves, their companies, and numerous business-friendly officials in the Fratbush regime. These were a few of the worst corporate decisions and their consequences: Big companies moved too many of their jobs to other countries, to save on taxes and wages, and this caused serious budget and unemployment problems in America; these global firms were also contributing greatly to a burgeoning trade imbalance as Americans bought far more goods overseas than they sold there; and, not least, the long-time employees of these American-based firms saw their pensions shrink as a consequence of such short-sighted and greedy company policies.

In this climate thrived a class of corporate thieves who blatantly stole millions in order to finance extravagant lifestyles. The courts eventually caught up with most of these white-collar criminals and sent them to prison. Perhaps the most notorious of them was Kenneth Pray, the founder of a corporation called Endrun (and one of the main contributors to the Bush-king machine). After his conviction but before he was to be sentenced, Ken Pray suffered a timely heart attack and died while still a free man.

Not all scandals in the corporate world were directly caused by the Fratbush regime, but some of the Ruler's own advocates and loyal followers did at times acknowledge that a climate of unregulated permissiveness encouraged such behavior. Industries that caused environmental pollution, such as coal mining and petroleum refining, found themselves less encumbered with rules than under previous leaders. The pharmaceutical industry was freer to set prices. The New York Stock Exchange, while barely keeping a break-even pace for average investors, was producing obscene profits for privileged insiders—confirming its well-established reputation as an American institution with no conscience and no memory.

The makers of war materiel got fast-track clearance that lowered government oversight and raised profits. Some favored corporations (such as Holyburton, previously headed by Dick Chaingang himself), subscribed to the axiom that war is good for business; they always managed to be near the front of the line when the government privatized and outsourced a wide range of service functions once handled by military personnel. These war profiteers worked hand-in-glove with a vast privatized propaganda machine to paint the Bush-king regime in the red, white, and blue colors of patriotism. Besides Holyburton, such names as Wackyhut, Bilgewater USA, the Carliar Group, Mangled Solutions, and N. Ron Benadores'ya were always in the forefront. And, helping to keep the wheels of government rolling smoothly for the benefit of the special interests was a veritable army of so-called lobbyists—free-enterprise partisans who literally bought the votes of Parliament members with cash and favors. In the Fratbush era, this parasitic task force more than doubled in size, to a number in excess of thirty thousand, creating a permanent encampment in an area of the Capital city known as the K Street corridor.

Many of the sins of omission and commission attributed to corporate and governmental function- aries during this time were clearly the fault of both political parties. Numerous desperately needed reforms that the Publicans under Fratbush fiercely resisted—universal health care, campaign finance and election practices, and controls over so-called "pork barrel" spending, to name three—were just as vigorously opposed by some in the Sinner Party. Sinners generally were almost as resistant to mean- ingful reform as Publicans, and fully deserved to share the blame for government inaction, no less than for misguided government action. Misfeasance and malfeasance of office in America's capital city was always a bipartisan affair.

When prices for gasoline and heating fuel soared,

Fratbush was properly faulted, but "market forces" were cited as the main cause, and no one seemed to know exactly who or what controlled those forces. In one brief but heated controversy, a plan to sell controlling interest in several American seaports to foreign investors brought a hail of criticism from Publicans and Sinners alike raining down upon the heads of the Bush-king directorate—but when the storm passed and the air cleared, no opponent of the transfer could offer a more satisfactory alternative. Foreign governments, it was pointed out, were buying up all manner of American properties, from bonds and real estate to entire industries, so why should ports be any different? True, there was a question of security, but no one knew how to close those gaps.

Paradoxically, however, security was the one promise above all others that Fratbush had repeatedly made to the American people since Nine-Eleven. "My first job," he told them, "is to protect you. There's a lot of danger and fear in this world, but just remember: Chaingang and Rumsfailed and I will keep you safe and secure. You can always count on us to do that." But years passed after the terrorist attacks, and the Department of Homeland Security spent tens of billions of dollars, and the secret police with alphabet names (FBI, CIA, NSA, etc.) read people's mail and looked at their private records and eavesdropped on their telephone conversations, and countless people were arrested and sent away without formal accusations of wrongdoing—and still, security remained loose and penetrable, as before. It may well be that security in a free society is a self-contradiction—an "oxymoron," in the common parlance of that time. In any case, it was not all Dubyiah's fault—but it was his responsibility, because the Constitution and the laws said so, and because he had publicly vowed to protect national security above all else.

Insoluble problems and widespread misbehavior that crossed party lines only reinforced the Bush-king's stubborn belief that his basic instincts were unerring, for the primary reason that they came to him directly, as a personal gift from God. Referring contemptuously to his critics, he drew gales of laughter from Babyface, Dr. Toughlove, and "Deadwood Dick" Chaingang when he made this sarcastic remark to them: "Next thing you know, they'll be blaming forest fires and tornadoes and hurricanes on me. 'Kill the messenger.' They just don't get it, do they? Only an ingrate—or a Sinner—would want to hold me responsible for an act of God."

It was beyond dispute that humans could not prevent acts of God—all they could do was suffer the blows and then address the consequences, for they could only be held accountable for their own actions. Fratbush, however, appeared to make no distinction between acts and consequences—both were God's doing, he said, and thus everything that he (the Ruler) thought and did had to be right, because he was merely a conduit through which the Almighty controlled the world.

By such logic, America's Ruler rationalized his behavior. It allowed him to admit no fault, but rather to declare proudly, "I say what I mean and mean what I say, and I am a man of my word, because it is really God's word that I am delivering."

And then, like a mighty shout from God, came Katrina.

Six.

Since the Great Flood that lifted Noah's Ark to the crest of Mount Ararat in ancient times, the world had known periodic devastation from the forces of Nature (which was another way of describing acts of God). In the early years of the third millennium, men and women of science were becoming alarmed by climate changes that seemed to foretell impending disaster, but not many leaders and policy makers appeared to take the warnings seriously. (One who did, ironically, was Prince Al Bore, the unfortunate victim of that turn-of-the-millennium election in which he defeated George Fratbush at the ballot box but lost the politically fraught split decision of the Supreme Court that put Fratbush and the Publicans in power; the Prince returned from exile near the end of the Ali

Dubyiah dynasty to deliver an "inconvenient truth" about global warming and other dire consequences of reckless disregard for the environment.) Catastrophic weather events happened more and more frequently—hurricanes, floods, tornadoes, earthquakes, volcanic eruptions, tidal waves, droughts, wildfires—and there was great destruction, and many people died. But then the sun came up again, and people cleared away the broken things as best they could, and in mourning they buried the dead and rebuilt. Life went on.

Within the first few years of the twenty-first century, all of these calamities befell one part of the globe or another, and more and more people witnessed this spreading arc of destruction with a hushed air of resignation. Further adding to the mood of pessimism was another kind of disaster, brought on by human failure: wars of scientific and technological madness, epidemics of fatal diseases, famine resulting from poverty and population density, and acts of genocide against entire populations of defenseless people. As these episodes of sprawling destruction mounted, it became increasingly difficult to muster an adequate emotional response;

more commonly, people simply looked away in passive silence, as if it were to become their destiny to witness the end of creation. (For some of the Fratbush religious fanatics, this was a consummation devoutly to be wished, for it would mark the beginning of the end of the world, according to their interpretation of the Apocalypse as described in the Book of Revelation in the Christian Bible.)

When Hurricane Katrina came ashore on an American coastline called Louisiana before dawn one summer morning, it was first thought that the city of New Orleans, squatting there in its path, had narrowly escaped a direct hit as the eye of the storm veered slightly to the east after making landfall. But then the manmade levees that kept the below-sea-level city in a protective bowl began to break under the pressure of so much water, and the bowl filled up, and New Orleans, with its half-million people, was left floating in a stagnant and polluted sea, like the sundered remains of a shipwreck. Hundreds drowned. Thousands escaped with nothing but the clothes they were wearing. The entire half-million, and millions more close to them, were forever changed, traumatized, by these twin blows from the inscrutable hand of God and the maladroit hand of man.

There was much more to be said about the terrifying catastrophe called Katrina, but aside from the physical and human destruction it caused, there was also a symbolic and philosophical and even theological lesson of great magnitude for the Fratbush regime to ponder and absorb. Just as Nine-Eleven happened only a few months after George the younger began his first term of national service, Katrina came along a few months into the start of his second term. Both were devastations that changed the course of American life. Whereas Nine-Eleven was entirely a manmade disaster, Katrina began as a force of nature, an act of God—but the flooding was a result of human failings, and so was the government response, which could charitably be described as casual ineptitude. Even more significantly, the Fratbush regime's handling of the Katrina crisis came to symbolize, then and forevermore, the utter failure of Ali Dubyiah's entire domestic performance, in much the same way that the invasion and occupation and ultimate destruction of Iraq represented the colossal failure of his foreign policy. Years into the future, the mere mention of President George W. Fratbush's name would elicit two words—Iraq, Katrina—that summed up the single most disastrous presidency in American history.

So many things went wrong in those years that it was next to impossible to keep them all sorted out. As a way of summarizing all the catastrophes, some scribes and scholars developed a "disaster index" to cluster problems and issues under various headings. For example, there was one widely used classification called "the Fratbush Doctrine." This was about America and its role in the world. In this category were included the wars, of course, but also the nation's attempt to forge a new global colonial empire, and its adversarial relationship with the Parliament of Nations, and international control of weapons of mass destruction, and the eternally thorny issue of immigration, and the phenomenon of economic globalization, and the booming market in sophisticated tools and weapons of war, and the relevance of international treaties and accords on topics ranging from treatment of war prisoners to protection of the environment. The need for a global strategy to deal with such matters as drug abuse, famine, agricultural technology, control of diseases, and the gaping contrasts of wealth and poverty also came under this general heading, this so-called Fratbush Doctrine. So many pressing problems urgently needed global solutions, but America in the Bush-age preferred to work alone, the better to control outcomes and protect its own self-interest—which was always consonant with the Ruler's conviction that he was being guided by the hand of God.

Another broad theme concerned the determination of Ali Dubyiah and his cabinet to fundamentally and radically change—more precisely, shrink—the role of the national government in the lives of its people. Under this heading was a long and ultimately dispiriting list of grossly inequitable policy reversals: steep cuts in the taxes paid by the wealthiest citizens, to the detriment of those with few assets; an abortive attempt to privatize the government's pension fund for the elderly, known as Social Security; a costly and unworkable prescription drug benefit program for elders, even as their existing health programs, called Medicare and Medicaid, were desperately in need of reform; special privileges and financial advantages for certain classes of industry, such as energy and pharmaceuticals; governmental education programs such as "No Child Left Behind," which proceeded to leave millions of poor and disabled children by the wayside, even as public funds were being redirected to support private and religious schools and social services; a generally dismal performance by government in such endeavors as public housing, job creation, minimum living wages, transportation, and criminal justice; and the so-called Patriot Act, hastily written by Fratbush operatives in the emotional wake of Nine-Eleven. It gave the government more power where it needed less—namely, to invade the privacy of citizens under a cloak of secrecy.

It was a long list, yet incomplete; indeed, there was no end to it. Here, in sum, was the heart and soul of what Fratbush considered his domestic platform of programs and services—and as he reached the three-quarter mark of his tenure in office, virtually the entire agenda was in some stage of disarray and dysfunction. And yet, paradoxically, his stated intention to shrink government and make it less of a factor in the lives of the people had produced precisely the opposite result: record spending, massive debts for future generations to pay, and far more intrusive federal meddling in private lives than ever was true under previous leaders of either party. If Fratbush had got his way, partisan government entities would have had the final word on such crucial and intimate personal matters as individual health decisions, public displays of religious and patriotic sentiment, the safeguarding of privacy, basic civil liberties, eligibility for marriage, and even matters of life and death.

A third major index of misdirected Bush-king policy initiatives was the radically altered relationship between government and religious institutions, and a fourth was the erosion of individual freedoms in the name of greater national security (when, in point of fact, it had been government secrecy that had worsened, while security seemed more porous and fragile after Nine-Eleven than before it). More such categories could be enumerated, but enough was already documented to underscore the central point: America and its federal government under

the second Bush-king was like a once-benevolent
beast, a gargantuan King Kong gorilla, driven to
erratic and destructive behavior by a ruthless cabal
of criminally irresponsible zookeepers.

I t would seem that all these failings on the Fratbush watch would have been more than enough
to drive him from office in disgrace (after common
sense and simple justice had failed to stop him outside the first gate). But three elections had come and
gone—his first, concluded but not resolved by the
Supreme Court under Sir William Inquest; then a
mid-term contest for many congressional seats; and
finally, his last close call in a carefully orchestrated
appearance before the national electorate—and
Fratbush was still clinging to power, with only two
more years left to serve before he would be required
by the Constitution to step down. His popularity
with the American people had all but evaporated.
Whereas more than nine in every ten had supported him after the attack by Osama bin Hiden's
secret cell of killers, barely one in three approved
of his conduct in office five years later. As the last
congressional election approached, Fratbush had

finally come into focus, even for many members of his own party: He was a divider, not a uniter or a "decider"—and more of a liability than an asset.

You may be wondering, then: Was the era of dominance by Bush-kings and Publicans entering its final days? Was there nothing left to be done with their tenure except a brief eulogy and a decent burial? Hardly. Since he himself could not stand for re-election and serve a third term as President, Ali Dubyiah was widely perceived as a so-called "lame duck," too weak to impose his will on Congress as he had freely done previously. But his natural instincts and personal tendencies were impervious to reality; he was the same arrogant, petty, dissembling, vindictive, partisan person he had always been. Worse, his destructive proclivities were now exaggerated by compulsions formed from the new realities that were facing him. Driven by a primitive instinct for survival and a desperate desire to influence the judgment of history, Fratbush focused every resource at his disposal upon salvaging his checkered career and trying to fashion a positive public recollection of his administration. (These were, in essence, so-called "public relations" tasks of the sort that he had previously left to his brain trust, but when he sensed the changed public mood and knew that time was running out, the Ruler became obsessed with manipulating the image of himself that would remain in the wake of his presidency.)

Dubyiah lived by professions, not principles. He professed faith and compassion, conservatism and self-reliance, but his principles belied those virtues. His principles were like reeds in the wind, blowing this way and that. To him, faith was meant to be blind and doubt-free, compassion was simply charity without empathy, and conservatism did not extend to such ideals as staying out of debt or keeping the Bill of Rights intact. As for self-reliance, that was fine, as long as there were others to do the heavy thinking for him. The moral compass of this shameless man was an unreliable tool that all too often led him—and thus the nation—astray.

These were not the qualities of a great leader. As he coasted toward the safe shore of retirement, Fratbush often seemed oblivious to the record of failure he had amassed, yet the hard truth was that he had committed more impeachable acts than any of his predecessors. His decision to invade Iraq was based upon assumptions, deceptions, and fabrications. At his bidding, or that of others assigned to do his bidding, a long string of falsified stories had emerged, intended in one way or another to conceal the truth—about Arab cooperation with (or resistance to) the invasion, about depleted Iraqi military power, about pre-arranged prisoner "rescues," about planted evidence and propaganda, about prisoner "rendition" and torture, about the sprawling terrorist insurgency that was using Iraq as a new training ground for desperados. Also deliberately concealed by the Fratbush high command: wrongful deaths (on both sides of the war), bribery, theft, profiteering, and the horrific toll of dead, wounded, and mentally shattered human beings (again, on all sides).

On the home front, Ali Dubyiah's mishandling of public funds, while perhaps not technically criminal, had the effect of criminality, causing as it did the loss of medical protection, pensions, jobs, community safety, and individual freedom for literally millions of citizens—as well as leaving future generations to pay for his errant profligacy. The wonder was not what qualities of individual and institutional resilience would be required to save the American nation from collapse; no, the wonder was what was keeping George W. Fratbush from being impeached, convicted, and sent to prison, or at least to premature retirement at his ranch in the western hinterlands.

The answer, in a word, was Sinners—to be precise, some of the most exalted members of the opposition Sinner Party. In the final analysis, it was they, not the Publicans, who saved the Bush-king from banishment.

During the stormy tenure of Fratbush's predecessor, King Zip, the Sinner Party had managed, even when its congressional majorities had evaporated, to steer their besieged leader past the hazardous reefs of impeachment and finally into calmer waters. As hard as they tried, the Publicans could not sink Zip, for the simple reason that too many of them were as vulnerable as he to charges of personal misconduct, and they knew with certainty that before he fell, he would drag them down with him.

With the second Bush-king, the shoe was on the other foot; Sinners who might have been able to force Ali Dubyiah to step down recognized that they were complicit in his false war and some of his fiascos at home, and he would surely make them share the burden of blame for those misdeeds. Thus, as was so often the case in the netherworld of politics everywhere (but transparently true in America), Fratbush found temporary salvation, not in the charmed circles where his customary allies gathered, but in the scattered outposts of his enemies, the Sinners. It was all quite predictable, and it brought to mind a saying heard widely in those days: "Bedfellows make strange politics." (Or was it the other way around?)

The Publicans, with their narrow majorities, might have been able to save their Ruler from impeachment with the help of only a few Sinners, but the verdict would have been too close for comfort. In any case, no Publican was overcome with anxiety or fear that an upheaval was remotely possible, for the Sinner Party was far too comfortable with the status quo and too compromised by its own behavioral history to stand on principle. As

national lawmakers, they were all, Publicans and
Sinners alike, members for life in the Congressional
Club, from whence came their pay and privileges
and a host of perquisites, not least being lifetime
medical care and retirement benefits as generous
as any socialist country would provide. None dared
jeopardize such taxpayer beneficence.

Further, their continuation as sitting lawmakers required their complicity in an arcane and
wastefully extravagant process of nominations,
campaigning, elections, boundary drawing, and
re-elections that defied all reason—but served
incumbents exceedingly well. In truth, only a
handful of these men and women seriously tried
to reform the election process in any way, whether
by reducing the cost of campaigning and elections,
or reapportioning districts more equitably, or
changing the ways in which ballots were recorded,
verified, counted, and made public. There were
many negative consequences to the system that
had evolved, but perhaps the worst was the direct
correlation between money and election. Hundreds
of millions of dollars were spent routinely to elect
presidents and senators and representatives. Only

the affluent could afford to seek office—and all too often, only the richest of them won.

There were other structural flaws that seduced incumbent Publicans and Sinners. Lobbyists offered them "amenities" in exchange for key votes on legislation, and many succumbed to the lures. Huge sums of tax money went annually to home-district projects of dubious merit, and these so-called "earmarks," or "pork-barrel" giveaways, winked at by the vast majority of senators and representatives, made a mockery of the concept of public service.

For reasons of self-interest (or fear of voter rejection), scores and even hundreds of the five hundred and thirty-five individuals who served in Congress found themselves lacking the courage to cast critically important but widely unpopular votes on a host of controversial issues, from reforms of health care, welfare, and Social Security pensions to revisions of the tax code and immigration laws. To cite one more glaring example: Trafficking and abuse of illegal drugs was a perennial scourge, just as price-gouging and market manipulation of legal prescription drugs was a constant outrage—yet the shamefully compromised houses of Congress, while never at a loss for words of indignant outrage, sat paralyzed and helpless for want of solutions to either problem.

An altogether different sort of compromise—one which involved earnest debate, advocacy tempered by empathy, and a give-and-take quest for solutions that realized the highest good for the greatest number—was a quality that all too few Sinners or Publicans manifested. So many vital issues cried out in vain for serious discussion and consensus. Separation of church and state, long thought to have constitutional protection, was under assault, and angry partisans traded shouts of defiance with their opposites on such emotionally-charged issues as abortion, capital punishment, self-realized sexual identity, environmental protection, universal health care, gun control, and family medical decisions. Still, neither party was willing to risk its tenuously held positions for the sake of reconciliation and unity.

Appointments to judicial and administrative positions were another bone of inter-party contention, no matter who was involved. But displays of breast-beating and feigned betrayal were not persuasive to thoughtful people who sat in witness of such histrionics; they knew from past observation that political chicanery was afoot. Everyone understood the rules: the President *pro*posed certain individuals for particular tasks, and the Senate *dis*posed of those nominations by voting to approve or reject them. To be sure, those whom Fratbush sent up to be confirmed brought out the worst in his Sinner adversaries in the Senate—but Publicans had exhibited the same hostility toward King Zip's appointees, and neither side had any genuine interest in much of anything except retribution for past grievances.

So much for bipartisanship on the domestic front. In the field of foreign affairs, brief acknowledgement of a few salient matters should be enough to show how intertwined the Sinners were with the political house that Ali Dubyiah had constructed in the sand.

First, there was Cuba, an island nation not even a day's float from this giant, America. During the consecutive regimes of nine Presidents—five Publicans, four Sinners—bitter hostilities had prevailed between these two countries. (America clung to a military base on one remote shoreline of Cuba, and it was there, ironically, that "enemy combatants" from Afghanistan and elsewhere had been caged and questioned at length by American officials, without legal counsel or formal charges, much to the consternation of human rights organizations around the world.) Against all common logic, diplomatic relations between Cuba and America could not be revived—and the Sinner Party was as much to blame for this as the Publicans. To this stalemate was appended the inability of any American administration to improve relations with most other western hemisphere nations, or to reduce the threat of nuclear proliferation worldwide, or to force an end to genocide bred by religion, race, and nationalism on the continents of Africa and Asia, or to reverse the trend of global warming and other environmental disasters.

All this evidence of Sinner complicity in the misdeeds of Ali Dubyiah could be clearly and convincingly seen without the necessity of mentioning the single most damning fact of all, namely this: The formal resolution authorizing the President

Fratbush to invade Iraq was approved in the lower House of Representatives months in advance of the war, by a vote of 296 to 133, and it also passed in the Senate, by a vote of 77 to 23. It was on the basis of these votes that Fratbush, as Commander in Chief, claimed not only to have the "advice and consent of Congress" to go to war, as the Constitution had been interpreted to require, but also to exercise the "war powers" that allowed him to spy, eavesdrop, and otherwise violate the privacy of American citizens in secret, without permission from any court.

In that climactic and ultimately decisive vote of the upper chamber, a clear majority of Sinner Party members—twenty-nine out of fifty—chose to cast their lot with Ali Dubyiah in support of the invasion. Among the most prominent of these "calculating patriots" were at least a dozen with burning political ambitions, either for another term in the Senate or a chance to replace Fratbush and Chaingang. They included Kerry Edwards and Edwards Kerry, later to be touted as a "dynamic duo" when they received their party's nominations for president and vice president; King Zip's zealous wife, Hillary-Tammy Rodham; Tom Dash-Elk, the party leader in the Senate, and Harry Reid-My-Lips, who later replaced him as leader; a rich Rockyfeller from poor West Virginia; Imbiben to Harken to Howlins to Bayh-Bayh, a smooth triple-play combination from Delaware, Iowa, South Carolina, and Indiana, respectively; and the California-Wisconsin-Connecticut-New York law firm of Finesheen, Kohltrain, Leiberschitz, and Schemer, who heard the call of the Israel lobby. To these wayward Sinners could be added the party's leader in the House, Dick Gepheartstrings. Without such willing accomplices, Fratbush and the Publicans could not have won congressional approval for their unilateral invasion of Iraq.

It was by then abundantly clear that neither American political party was willing to put world or even national interests ahead of their personal political survival. And that, in sum, was all the proof anyone ever needed to establish, beyond a shadow of a doubt, that the Sinner Party would never seriously attempt to impeach George W. Fratbush, or even vote to censure him with a resolution of disapproval; his manifest and manifold high crimes and misdemeanors would go unpunished.

not least of these sins, lest it be forgotten, was Katrina. She had come like a howling ghost in the night, and had departed swiftly, leaving death and destruction in her wake. Four days later, Fratbush approached cautiously to the outer perimeter. Two weeks after that, he returned to stand in the glare of television floodlights in the heart of New Orleans and make these assertions and promises to a rapt nation:

"We will do whatever it takes to rebuild . . . do it quickly, honestly, wisely . . . make it better and stronger than before the storm. . . In partnership with the states and the cities, the Federal Government will lead this reconstruction effort . . . over sixty billion dollars is already committed, and there will be more, whatever it takes . . . There is no way to imagine America without New Orleans, and this great city will rise again."

A year later, New Orleans and most of the central coast of the Gulf of Mexico, from east Texas to west Florida, still lay prostrate and broken, and few if any of the Ali Dubyiah promises had been kept. Incompetent and corrupt government officials had stolen or otherwise wasted billions of tax dollars. New Orleans was America's domestic Iraq, a constant reminder of the wrath of God and the folly of man—this man Fratbush and his band of outlaws in particular.

In ancient times, before the rise of Babylonia, a biblical prophet named Hosea may have said it best: "They have sown the wind, and they shall reap the whirlwind."

Seven.

If there was one virtue that George W. Fratbush possessed above all others, it was loyalty. He did not desert his compatriots, friends, colleagues, or family in times of stress. But some left him—in fact, many did: Werewolf, Sackcloth, Colin O'Scoppy, Andy Holecard (his chief of staff), advisers and cabinet members such as treasury secretary Paul O'Migosh, environmental protector Christie Whitewoman, neocolonialism expert Richard Perlehandle, and counter-terrorism specialist Richard Clarke-Shark. Fratbush also wore out two press secretaries, Airy Flasher and Scott McCome-Clean, before he recruited Tony Snowjob, a seasoned scrivener with the Fox War Channel, to replace the casualties. (Snowjob beat out former Iraqi information minister Mohammed Saeed al-Sahaf for the job.)

Still others would not be with him at the end, including General Tommy Hotdog, Viceroy Paul Tremor, and so-called "chief spook" George "Slam Dunk" Tenant. His replacement as director of the CIA was called, appropriately, Porter Ghost; this former congressman served only briefly before his fleeting image dissolved into that of the next high spy: Sterling Hayden, a real general (who, it was rumored, had once portrayed a make-believe general in an anti-war movie). Fratbush's party chieftains, Tom DeCeive and Bill Frisk, both under a legal cloud, were to end up doing the Ruler more harm than good, as did a full theater of retired generals and admirals who publicly criticized their Commander in Chief. DeCeive's departure was especially telling; he resigned from Congress after a grand jury in his home state of Texas indicted him on criminal charges of conspiring to violate campaign finance laws. This list lengthened measurably in the last three years of the regime, and when only a few fresh horses could be corralled to replenish the herd, Fratbush's stable shrank to the size of a camel's hump. Finally, only a handful of die-hard loyalists stood by him (in mind and spirit, if not in the flesh): Chaingang, Rumsfailed, Condi Pasta, and the ever-faithful Machiarovelli —who, along with Chaingang's resigned chief of staff, Scooter Libby-Lobby, was the focus of a grand jury investigation into the criminal exposure, for political reasons, of an American spy. The babyfaced one eventually managed to slip free of that noose, leaving the unfortunate Scooter to stand trial alone, on charges of perjury and obstruction of justice.

These were among the most newsworthy individuals to jump or be pushed from high places in the Fratbush administration, not by any means a complete list. Other Bush-king associates with close ties to confessed influence peddler Jack "The Ripper" Abramon were also indicted in the wake of the lobby king's guilty plea, and that scandal grew into one of the biggest to touch the White House in a generation. Many Publicans ran for cover when Abramon became an untouchable pariah in Washington, but for some—like DeCeive—it was too late to avoid the Ripper's embrace. (Once, in a public declaration of undying loyalty and praise,

Abramon declared: "Tom DeCeive is who we all
want to be when we grow up.")

Throughout this exodus, Dubyiah's loving Librarian stood by her man—she was his rock—but
toward the end, he was a lonely soul. This had
befallen others before him, but none had felt it so
acutely—except perhaps King Richard the Cold-
Hearted. The thought of these two embattled kings
in deep misery underscored a poignant truth about
both: in their anguished decline, they were faithfully
supported only by a few loyal women whose influence was limited—and dragged down by men of
surpassing power and vanity who posed as selfless
patriots, when in fact they were pursuing their own
selfish agendas. Foremost among these duplicitous
counselors to Ali Dubyiah were Chaingang and
Rumsfailed—the one a white-collar schemer whose
least crime had been the careless shooting of a fellow hunter during an alcohol-lubricated safari, and
the other a megalomaniac who gleefully played the
deadly game of war with no rules except those he
made up as he went along.)

The last election Dubyiah had to endure came
in the sixth year of his reign, when all seats in the

House of Representatives and one-third of those in the Senate were subject to review by the citizenry. The Publicans had by then enjoyed the upper hand in Congress for more than a decade—long enough to give Ali Dubyiah a cocky attitude of smug satisfaction that his Sinner adversaries found maddening, and even some Publicans knew was riskily provocative.

Previously, following his re-election triumph, he had arrogantly crowed that his narrow victory gave him a mandate and a wealth of political capital that he intended to exploit. But two years later, with the wars going badly and his domestic agenda in tatters, public opinion polls were showing major slippage in the Ruler's base of hard-core voters (those whose strong approval of his performance in office had never wavered). Whereas nearly half of all poll respondents had voiced such extremely favorable sentiments before the previous election, less than one in four did so as the last balloting neared.

But this worrisome disadvantage to the Bush-king machine was muted by the influence of a peculiar election feature with an utterly baffling name: "gerrymandering." The configuration of

House districts was periodically adjusted according to law, so that each would have an equitable number of voters. Gerrymandering was a time-honored but otherwise dishonorable manipulation of the voter profile; its effect was to make most House districts strongly favor one party or the other, thus leaving very few in which truly competitive contests were possible. Both parties were equally to blame for resorting to this two-century-old travesty against true democracy.

The tool had worked to Dubyiah's advantage in the previous elections, with the Publicans consistently maintaining a majority of ten to thirty seats over the Sinners in the House of Representatives. But when the last election of his reign was over and the votes were counted, that margin had evaporated, leaving the representation of the two parties almost evenly divided in the chamber of four hundred and thirty-five seats.

Over in the Senate, where reapportionment was not a factor, Publicans had attained parity at the start of the Fratbush regime, and actually had gone on to open up a ten-vote advantage (fifty-five seats to forty-five in opposition) in the same election that returned the Ruler to office. But that "politi-cal capital," as Dubyiah had called it, was soon squandered by him and his band, and in the final round of polling, the Sinners recouped enough of their prior losses to end, like the House, in a virtual deadlock with the Publicans (practically speaking, a fifty to fifty standoff on most legislation).

No doubt those election results were encourag-ing to the Sinners, who registered solid gains for the first time in many years—and equally dismaying to the Publicans, who previously had lost nothing of importance at the ballot box since Ali Dubyiah came to power. But as a practical matter, it was bad news for both, for it pushed the government deeper into stalemate. A lame duck was on the throne, the evenly-divided legislative branch was full of insignificant sound and fury, and the High Court and its lower branches were afflicted with the same sort of partisan paralysis.

Not surprisingly, the last two Bush-king years were filled with high drama. Battle-scarred old warriors and hot-blooded newcomers clashed like gladiators in a life-and-death ordeal. The Ruler, who had come to power calling himself "a uniter, not a divider," was now declaring, "I am the decider," and his lofty disdain for the views of others set the tone for one of the most contentious and destructive legislative sessions in the history of the American Congress. This once-noble deliberative body, long having prided itself on its civility, comity, diplomacy, and bipartisan spirit, was reduced to a raucous mob, its energy spent in shameful public displays of empty fulmination and impotent rage.

Within the American nation, other non-political signs of disintegration had begun to surface. The people were losing their positive spirit, their active nature, their industriousness, their openness, their sense of confidence; even their identity was at risk, for they lived and died by electronic transactions and communications, and thieves had learned to steal their numerical profiles and convert them to material riches. Americans had become obese and soft from inactivity and overindulgence; they had lost their zest for physical exertion, choosing instead to be watchers, not doers. It seemed inevitable, then, that citizens in ever-expanding numbers would abandon their civic duties and retire to the sidelines to be voyeurs at such artificially stimulating activities as sporting events, sexually titillating picture shows, and the ultimate bloodsport, politics. Manual labor was another thing that a declining number of people were willing to do; machines now did much of the work that formerly had to be done by hand—and what machines could not do, eager immigrants were there to fill the void. Not just the affluent but even many marginal people—unskilled, unemployed, unmotivated—shunned hard work at any pay.

By the same token, civic-minded participation in local affairs was also on the decline. Few were drawn any longer to debate the Fratbush foreign policy or his domestic reforms, such as they were; those opportunities had long since dissolved into thin air, like so much empty rhetoric. Throughout the last two years of his regime, the only forward-facing thoughts to surface among the citizenry were typically articulated as vague hopes, something close to prayers, that George W. Fratbush's last days in office would somehow pass without utter catastrophe, and that he would quietly return to his ranch in the western territory, from whence he had been snatched up by fate and installed for eight harrowing years at the helm of the world's most powerful nation.

And that is what eventually happened, though the details were fraught with anxiety and peril. Those who had hoped for a decisive turn toward recovery and peace, once the Bush-king syndicate had been replaced, would be bitterly disappointed to see the Publicans and the Sinners recklessly alternating one-term presidents into and out of the big White House in Washington City for the next four or five presidential elections, with third-party candidates from the left and right in hot pursuit—and by that time, so much was in disintegration and chaos that the selection of America's leader and his or her effectiveness were no longer matters of paramount importance to the electorate, which grew smaller with each successive campaign.

Ali Dubyiah's "end time" bore no resemblance to the "rapture" his radical band of Christian Right prophets had so confidently heralded. In fact, reality turned out to be just the opposite of what all self-proclaimed "messianic liberators"

were expecting. Instead of ascending to an idyllic
and timeless Kingdom of Paradise, there to dwell
forever among the Chosen, they were left behind
to sift through the wreckage of human failure and
gaze in utter disbelief upon an apocalypse hastened
by their narcissistic pride and self-righteousness.

The mighty clock of earthly time was ticking
inexorably. All civilizations before America had
crumbled, each one having climbed, as it were,
upon the shoulders of its predecessors and stood
there, reaching for the stars, until it fell of its own
weight. And so it would be with America. The
immutable law of gravity was once again in force
and applicable. All history sinks. Things in motion
come to rest. *Sic transit gloria mundi.*

From our own distant vantage point in time,
almost a thousand years after these things happened, the signs of impending doom that were
bearing down upon this cloud-plumed blue orb
in those portentous days now seem crystal clear
to us: extremes of advantage and disadvantage
stretching ever wider between peoples, resulting in
economic collapse and political anarchy; global climate change and other natural phenomena creating

environmental no-go zones; manmade catastrophes such as uncontrolled population swings, runaway technologies, and globally rampant diseases; wars begetting more wars, with the specter of annihilation ever present and menacing; and the failure of institutions, kindled by the loss of trust in government and the loss of faith in religion. It would take a full century or more for all those forces in combination to bring about the present condition of life on Earth, here at the night-darkened end of the third millennium.

In the days of Ali Dubyiah and the Forty Thieves, few people could recognize these approaching dangers, and none could know how soon they would be felt or when it would be too late to stop them. It is in the nature of the human animal to gaze narrowly, to think and act selfishly, to hesitate past the most propitious moment. Empires, like individual members of the species *Homo sapiens*, have tended in the main to die gradually—of starvation or consumption, blocked arteries, implosion, self-inflicted wounds. The rest, for the most part, have died suddenly, violently—if not one by one, at the hands of their enemies, then many at once, by planned extinction with weapons of mass destruction.

America gives us the clearest example of these somber principles. For all its wealth and abundance, its good fortune, its intellectual qualities, its strong institutions, its decent citizens, this blessed society only lasted four or five centuries. Its eventual demise was energized (accidentally? intentionally? avoidably? inevitably?) by the same forces at work in the larger world since the beginning of time: forces of nature, forces beyond our comprehension, and the collective forces of a flawed and imperfect species, committing acts of heroism and stupidity, intentionally and at random.

It all seemed to work, somehow—or, more precisely, did not cease to work somehow—until the fossil fuels were used up or shut off, and the electricity failed, and the machines stopped.

Eight.

s I said at the beginning, these things happened long ago and far away, in a time and
place that seers and scholars would come to
describe as the apex of the human journey—the
mountaintop, the pinnacle. Not to suggest that
so-called "Western civilization" was necessarily
superior to the Eastern cultures, of course—it
was not—but America and Europe had enjoyed
a period of such wealth and abundance and
creativity that they could afford to spare no cost
in the development of modern innovations. In a
period of approximately five centuries—that would
be from around the year 1500 to about the year
2000—Europeans, joined in time by Americans,
recorded great advancements in numerous fields
of endeavor. Men and women learned to generate
heat and light from sources other than fire, to build

magnificent new structures, to travel at great speeds by means of various conveyances, to fly in the sky, to live underwater and far off into space. There was no end to their clever inventions. In a single hundred-year period, from the middle of the 1800s to the middle of the 1900s, these pioneers learned to create electric power that provided artificial light, and to build vehicles with engines that got their strength from liquefied petroleum and other refined fuels. These ingenious machines led in turn to voice transmittal over long distances, soon to be followed by pictures and sound that people in one place could send instantly to people elsewhere. Radio and television, so-called computers for transmitting information at astonishing speeds, automobiles and airplanes, steamships and submarines, long trains that hauled freight as well as people, trucks and buses that did the same on highways, all manner of electric and battery-operated conveyances and appliances, even rocket ships that sped travelers to the moon and the planets! We can hardly imagine such things now.

To speak of this as a climb to the mountaintop seems especially apt, for its profile on a scale resembles such: a long, gradual ascension from a darkened plain to a succession of plateaus, each higher than the one before, until at last the pinnacle is reached and maintained for a brief period—after which the descent begins, gathers speed, bumps downward in stairstep fashion, and finally levels out once again in a shallow pool of darkness. This is how that arc might look, drawn upon a papyrus scroll:

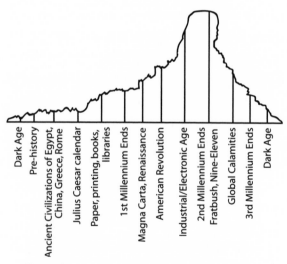

Over the course of recorded history, this trajectory shows as a slow ascension, a gradual rise, for about five thousand years, beginning with the origination of language, and a more precipitous fall over the last thousand years or so. Periodic escalations were caused by the introduction of some new force—horses, iron, ships, wheels, guns, atoms—and civilizations rose, from Mesopotamia (Oh, Babylon!) and Egypt to Athens and Rome. But those empires eventually fell, and each time, the rising mountain of human progress lost altitude, only to regain it and reach new heights.

Just three thousand years ago, the Roman emperor Julius Caesar introduced the calendar that would mark the turning of the seasons, years, and centuries. Halfway between that time and this— around the year 1500—a great burst of creative and material advancement began, and it lasted, as I have suggested, for about five hundred years. But even as this civilizational growth was accelerating, the seeds of its own destruction were being sown: greed, waste, insensitivity, slavery, hate, violence, war, and so on.

In the last decades before the second millennium (on the Caesar calendar) drew to a close, these human flaws had begun to overtake the good qualities in humanity, but few people took notice. Finally, a pinnacle was reached, but no one realized it, or knew that the descent of humanity was beginning. It has continued now, with increasing speed, for the past thousand years.

Someone once likened history to the incessant crashing of ocean waves against a cliff. For centuries, nothing happens. Then—suddenly, as it were—the cliff collapses and falls into the sea. America, and the other great civilizations before it, did not quite fall into the sea—but even as their power was at its zenith, disintegration was already at work, and when the fall came, it must have seemed precipitous to those who stood at the top. From such a long perspective as ours, this pattern that I have just outlined for you has a certain beauty, a natural shape and form, but in the living of it—from ashes to ashes, dust to dust, darkness to darkness—it has never been without its stormy clouds of agony and dread, however much the better moments sometimes shone through.

The brief reign of Ali Dubyiah and the Forty Thieves was not one of the brighter moments in this history. It lasted only eight years, a mere flicker in the candlelight of time, but it was momentous in that it marked the tipping over from the arduously attained crest to the gradually descending slope. For the feckless Ruler himself—George W. Fratbush, the President, the man who would be King—the whole catastrophe no doubt lingered on in his memory like a thousand years of solitude as he puttered through his twilight period in self-exile on the ranch where his dreams of glory had first taken wing. True, he still had fences to mend there, and brush to clear, all the way to the distant horizon; he would never run out of "hard work." But even as he bent to those labors and pushed his wistful recollections to the outer edges of memory, the questions must have hovered there, lurking like stealthy bandits, whispering to him from the shadows and, ever so gradually, spiriting away his frail peace of mind:

How is it possible that America is not a major player in the Middle East anymore? In the world!? Hell, if it's any consolation, nobody's *a major player in the world! China? No way . . . not enough oil . . . Same old song . . . heard that one before, haven't we? . . . huh? Like, "Hu's on first?" Heh, heh . . .*

Far as you can see out here, nothin' but scrub oaks and mesquite, dust and tumbleweeds . . . Damn, it's hot! . . . Yeah, yeah, okay, I know the joke by now, and I'm sick of it . . . global warming, my ass! People are so stupid, they don't know a heat wave from a hurricane. . . . I've seen it worse in my day, a lot worse!

This is how Lyndon ended up, out here by himself . . . I used to laugh my ass off at that old goat . . . a pitiful sight, tryin' to rehabilitate himself before the Lord and the liberals and the historians. Well, damn 'em all—except the Lord, of course. Heh, heh . . . Yeah, I laughed hard at LBJ . . . I'm not laughin' all that hard now . . . heh.

But by God, it wasn't my fault! We had a plan, a vision—it's just that a lot of people let us down: insubordinate generals and admirals . . . media vultures . . . rabid pack of self-righteous Sinners . . . Publican traitors, too . . . and that Rapture crowd, what a bunch of leeches! They were sendin' the wrong signal . . . hell, I'd rather *be left behind than get trapped in eternity with all those assholes!*

But there it is, dammit, no way around it . . . Iraq's been bogged down in civil war since before I left Washington . . . Syria and Lebanon fightin' again . . . Israelis and the Palestinians—how long's that been goin' on, a hundred years? . . . Turks, Pakistanis, Saudis, Egyptians . . . Boy, when I talked about "You're either with us or you're with the terrorists," I had to keep my fingers crossed behind my back for that two-faced bunch of shaky sheiks, huh? . . . sneaky snakes, heh, unh!

And would you believe, heh, I just stood here and almost forgot to mention Afghanistan? . . . And Iran, of all places! Talk about your religious fanatics, Iran's crawlin' with 'em, has been ever since I was a kid . . . Remember when they kidnapped a bunch of our people back when Carter was president? Hunh? Kept 'em for over a year! No shit! . . . Wasn't totally a bad thing, though, huh . . . cause it put Reagan in the White House. Huh, huh?

It gets confusin' . . . Muslims and Islam, that's the same thing, right? But there's Sunnis, there's Shiites, there's Kurds—who are not Arabs, but . . . but what? And then you got your African and Asian Muslims . . . and what about North Korea? What are they, Buddhists or something? Or nothing? Huh?

That guy Kim, I gotta admit—that guy had balls! He was a true nutcase—looked like Steve Allen in a bad wig, playin' some Asian character on TV—but the little fella had absolutely no fear! We shoulda took him out first, asked questions later. Same with that little terrorist bastard in Iran . . .

What went wrong *over there? Rumsfailed and Chain-gang were so positive Iraq would be quick and easy—"shock and awe," they told me. "A slam dunk." (Or was that Tenant? Or Condi?)*

When Saddam's statue came tumblin' down in Baghdad, we already had a sculptor workin' on a heroic likeness of me—"The Liberator," heh—to go up in that same square. My handlers kept tellin' me, "You're the Man, you're MacArthur and Patton and Tommy Hotdog, all condensed into one kick-ass commando, one wily desert fox—the War President, the one and only Commander in Chief!"

We had a brilliant game plan . . . I never doubted the outcome, not once, not even when our losses were higher than predicted. Then we caught that bastard Saddam—jerked his sorry ass up out of a hole in the ground like some shit-eatin' cockroach, and I thought then, and kept right on thinkin', "It's all workin' out according to plan—I've caught this butcher who got away from my father, and we've got us a permanent base in the Middle East, and enough oil to end our worries, and we're gonna turn this sandpile into a Christian democracy . . . The Publicans will rule for a thousand years, and I'll go down in history as the first Emperor of the World, a compassionate conservative . . . hand-picked by God himself."

"Those were the days, my friend, we thought they'd never end . . ."

But then, you're always gonna have terrorists and traitors to deal with, and I had more than my share. People have to understand: We gave Iraq every chance to put up a friendly democracy in place of the Gomorrah dictatorship, but they just couldn't get their act together. Hell, we bought and paid for the whole thing—constitution, parliament, judiciary, executive branch—every detail modeled on our system. And look what they did with it: couldn't even manage to condemn Saddam to death and hang the bastard from a high limb for all the world to see . . . I bet if he had renounced Islam and told 'em he was convertin' to Christianity, they'd have chopped his head off so fast he wouldn't have known it 'til he tried to turn around and wipe his ass! Huh? Heh, heh.

That's life, though, isn't it? What was it Forrest Gump's mama told him in that movie? "Life is like a box of chocolates, Forrest—you never know what you're gonna get." I loved that movie . . . Ol' Forrest, he was a funny guy. "You never know what you're gonna get." Heh.

Just like Katrina—nobody ever imagined the levees would break, and New Orleans would fill up like a bathtub—but that's what happened.

Now why do you suppose God let it happen?

That's the part that's really hard for me to understand, and I've never had anybody I could talk to about it—not even Babyface, for all his Christian expertise. I mean, there's God, working his will through me, and here comes all these "acts of God," these natural disasters, one after another . . . a tidal wave in Southeast Asia, a huge earthquake up in the mountains of Pakistan . . . (Suppose that could have been a God-strike against al Qaida, just a little off target?) . . . and forest fires everywhere, some close enough that I could stand out here on my back forty and close my eyes and breathe real deep, and I could smell *'em! . . . tornadoes . . . floods . . . hurricanes . . .*

And Katrina. I'll never get over that. Just when I'd been re-elected and was getting' my agenda up and runnin', and it was time to be workin' on my presidential library, my legacy . . . and look out, here it comes, the shit hits the fan! Katrina, Rita, Shirtoff and Brownie, Nagin and that woman governor, what's her name . . . Louisiana political assholes, big time . . . and everybody and his mangy dog wantin' to blame me *for the whole mess!*

I really felt betrayed by all the people that turned against me . . . Still do . . . We had everything all lined up, overseas and over here—the baksheesh-lovin' Arabs, the weapons makers, the big-money boys, the super-patriots, the "Moral

Majority," *the corporate monopolists, Wall Street and Main Street . . . Libertarians and Catholics, Evangelicals and Whiskeypalians . . . the cheap-labor pool, foreign investors . . .*

So you tell me: How could we have had all that—and now here I am, out here clearin' brush, just me and my Secret Service detail? . . . No more important visitors, favor-seekers, media whores . . . just me and God, mendin' fences on the high lonesome . . .

I wonder what you were thinkin', God . . . Not tryin' to be a smartass, uh, acting disrespectful or anything, just wonderin' . . . Hunh.

Maybe He was tryin' to tell me somethin'. I really do wonder . . .

And you know what else? After all these years, there's another thing I still wonder about. Matter of fact, I think about this a lot, 'cause I'd really like to know, huh? . . . I wonder . . . whatever became of Osama bin Hiden?

Presenter's Afterword

I n the early autumn of 1889, J. A. Mitchell, a
prominent New York City editor and writer,
ushered into print through the publishing house
of Frederick A. Stokes & Brother a slender volume
of fantasy and satire called *The Last American*. It
followed the exploits of a band of Persians who
sailed out of the Middle Ages on a wooden ship,
crossed the seas and the centuries, and arrived in
New York harbor in the year 2951.

To their astonishment, they discovered there
the silent ruins of a collapsed and abandoned
culture—a "lost civilization," to use the phrase
that many novelists and readers in Mitchell's time
found so alluring. Clearly, he was riding a popular
wave of creative imagination, but his aim was not
merely to entertain. Through something akin to

135

literary triangulation, John Ames Mitchell tried to blend the remote past with the distant future to arrive at a tightly focused and critical picture of the society in which he lived. It is difficult—maybe impossible—to determine to what extent he succeeded, but his effort alone is more than enough to invite imitation.

The late nineteenth century was a fruitful season for the popular literary genre known as science-fiction. After the French fantasist Jules Verne published *20,000 Leagues Under the Sea* in 1869 (the third of four major works by him in a span of eight years), a rush of imaginative adventure tales soon followed, bending time and space in every direction. In the same decade that Mitchell delivered *The Last American*, three British-born novelists produced titles that would make them famous: Robert Louis Stevenson's *Treasure Island*, H. Rider Haggard's *King Solomon's Mines*, and H. G. Wells's *War of the Worlds*.

Readers happily devoured such tales, and writers were eager to feed their appetites. It was as if a bond had been made between reader and writer to suspend the laws of time and space, just to see what could be made of such freedom. The rationale for removing these constraints went something like this (couched in contemporary terms):

We are accustomed to living within a single plane of time that stretches back in a straight line to the beginning—that is to say, to the earliest recorded human act. From where we are now, in the twenty-first century of "modern" time, we can "see" thousands of years into the past, simply by looking at the uncovered and preserved drawings, symbols, and shapes that primitive cave dwellers etched in stone.

But powerful evidence (albeit anecdotal) suggests that there are now, and have always been, other planes or bands or layers of time that are elastic and reversible, and within those bands it is possible to move at will through space and across time.

People who have known time only in the conventional way—that is, as past tense (which we commonly call "memory" or "history") and as present tense (which is our conscious state from moment to moment)—tend to be skeptical of these other planes of existence. Nonetheless, it seems fair to say that most people in the world of today do have a way of thinking about time in the future tense. Their response to the mystery of an unknown and unknowable future perhaps can be captured best in a single word: religion.

Every major religious faith since the beginning of time has been rooted in an acceptance, reached only through a leap of faith, that an eternal life of happiness is the reward that awaits believers after they die. To put it another way, the generally accepted divisions of time—past, present, future—are functionally synonymous with three capacities common to all sentient human beings: memory, consciousness, and faith (which, for many, is an elevated expression of hope).

It would be pointless to try to persuade or convince those who deny the possibility of time travel that it is either more or less susceptible to proof or disproof than is religious faith. The question is not whether the existence of such travel can be proven (or, for that matter, the existence of God, by whatever name). These are matters for physicists and theologians to ponder, not readers of fantasy. For readers to absorb a good science-fiction story, there is only one imperative: a suspension of disbelief. Instead of saying, "Such a thing is impossible," we have to say, "What if it were true?"—that space ships can soar from one age to another, that civilizations can exist beneath the sea, that people can render themselves invisible. What if?

Such was the reasoning, more or less, and it worked spectacularly when writers like Verne and Wells addressed their readers—as it had worked for Jonathan Swift, who wrote *Gulliver's Travels* a century and a half before them. And, on a more modest scale, it also worked for John Ames Mitchell. *The Last American* was reprinted at least a dozen times and stayed in print for two decades. In its essence—and, no doubt, in the darkly humorous imagination of its author—the book was more than a quaint fable about turbaned Persians encountering the dead Western world at the end of the third millennium; its energy and passion arose from Mitchell's firm conviction that his New York and his America were careening toward catastrophe. His era would come to be called the Gilded Age, a time of hedonistic extravagance, and Mitchell saw it as a forecast of a gathering storm that would bring disaster.

Surrounded as he was by the ostentatious self-indulgence of the Robber Barons of high society, Mitchell found plenty of targets for his stinging arrows of social judgment. Curiously, his protagonists looked and talked like sixteenth-century refugees from the Ottoman Empire as they gazed upon the empty stone canyons of thirtieth-century New York and Washington. They also called one another by quirkily humorous names—No-fuhl and Ad-el-pate and Ja-khaz. And yet, with surprising force, their observations and conversations spoke directly to the pervasive excesses of the rich and powerful in Mitchell's time—and they still ring true in ours.

The Last American, soon to be a hundred and twenty years old, is a modest little gem that retains its luster and its cutting edge, a small treasure rescued from the sands of time. It is an inspiration and a worthy model for *Ali Dubyiah and the Forty Thieves*—a timeless fable that rightly belongs to no author, but to all the readers and tellers who find meaning in it, identify with it, and even think of it as theirs because it expresses the way they feel.

The stories and characters in this fable are different, of course, but its most salient features—moveable time and space—are the same as before, and so is the long perspective: travelers from the east striving to understand, from a vantage point far in the future, how and when and why America ("sweet land of liberty," "the land of the free and home of the brave") fell from grace. These were questions that few dared ask when John A. Mitchell lived and wrote in New York a century ago. Here in the first decade of the twenty-first century, they remain among the central questions to be answered in our time.

Postscript

The fable *Ali Dubyiah and the Forty Thieves* stands alone as a complete story in these pages, but it was conceived as an integral part of a more complex work of imagination and history to be called *Western Voyages*. The first half of *Western Voyages* will consist of J. A. Mitchell's novel, *The Last American*, originally published in New York in 1889. A facsimile edition of *The Last American* is available now. For more information, please visit: www.newsouthbooks.com/westernvoyages. At that same site will be found information on the progress and availability of the sequel, called "Return to America," which incorporates the Ali Dubyiah tale within its narrative.

Ali Dubyiah and the Forty Thieves, first published in August 2006, is available in the original hardcover edition at bookstores throughout the United States, and may also be found on the Internet—in book form, as an audio compact disk, and as a downloadable ebook. For more information or to engage in discussion about the content of the book and the background of the 1889 fable which inspired it, visit the book's website, www.newsouthbooks.com/alidubyiah.